THE AMERICAN TABLE

CLASSIC COMFORT FOOD FROM ACROSS THE COUNTRY

CHEF LARRY EDWARDS

Skyhorse Publishing

THE AMERICAN TABLE

Skyhorse Publishing books may be purchased in bulk at special discounts for sales promotion, corporate gifts, fund-raising, or educational purposes. Special editions can also be created to specifications. For details, contact the Special Sales Department, Skyhorse Publishing, 307 West 36th Street, 11th Floor, New York, NY 10018 or info@skyhorsepublishing.com.

Skyhorse® and Skyhorse Publishing® are registered trademarks of Skyhorse Publishing, Inc.®, a Delaware corporation.

Visit our website at www.skyhorsepublishing.com.

10 9 8 7 6 5 4 3 2 1

Library of Congress Cataloging-in-Publication Data is available on file.

Cover design by Jane Sheppard
Cover photography by iStockphoto
Interior photography by Casa de Cuisine

Print ISBN: 978-1-5107-2152-4
eBook ISBN: 978-1-5107-2153-1

Printed in China

Table of Contents

Introduction

When it comes to food, either cooking or eating, American fare is more than "amber waves of grain." Like the people who make up this beautiful mass of land we call the United States of America, true American food is a melting pot of taste and texture. True American food harkens back to slavery and dishes brought to America from Africa, the West Indies, and other countries involved in the slave trade. True American food is adaptations of dishes from the southern regions of our borders and, in many cases, from the northern regions. True American food has its origins in Asia and Europe, brought to this wonderful land of liberty by immigrants looking for a better way of life. In a very real way, true American food is the epitome of world culinary history.

True American food is a goulash pot of earthy goodness, stirred together with imagination and served with pride. It is red, white, and blue—and just for good measure, a few rainbows thrown in for extra flavor. American food is more than some dishes from the South. American food is the freshness from the vineyards of California. It is the vibrant flavors of New England. It is the tongue tantalizers of the great American Southwest. It is a plate full of East Coast goodness. It is the robust nature of the Midwest, and yes, it features the "amber waves of grain" from the Great Plains.

Whereas many international cuisines take a great deal of pride in keeping their native foods historically accurate, you will never really find this to be the case with American food. Why? Because American food is the epitome of bastardization. This is not a bad thing. As a matter of fact, it is a good thing. American food is ever-changing. What is cooked one way today will probably see an adaptation tomorrow. American food is an idea which just seems to deliciously grow. A perfect example of this is American eateries in general and the famed American diners, truck stops, cafés, and roadside eateries in particular. As a matter of fact, it is within the walls of the aforementioned eating establishments where American food really shines its brightest.

If you have ever traveled the roads of this beautiful country of liberty, you have no doubt stopped at more than a few roadside eateries. Whether they were called diners, truck stops, or cafés, if you ate there, you experienced Americana. Though there are many American homes which celebrate true American food with recipes handed down through generations, it is the roadside eateries which keep our culinary history alive. Sure, they may have some of the latest chic and fad fare, but you can bet your Uncle Sam hat, they will also feature some dishes which are a part of their cooking history. It may be fried chicken. It may be chili. It may be pot roast. It may even be the fabled (and oftentimes cursed) cream-chipped beef, which also has the rather colorful moniker of "shit on a shingle." No matter what they may put on your plate, it will be pure Americana with possibly a dash of originality, just to keep your mouth honest.

As we venture throughout America via the pages of this book, you will notice something rather interesting. Long before there was the rage (or fad) of using fresh products, it was a staple of the American kitchens. When you needed vegetables, fruits or fresh herbs, you simply went into your yard and picked them. If you didn't have them, chances are very strong your neighbor did. If you had to venture to the market, their produce sections usually only consisted of locally grown produce. My, how things have changed. Along these same lines, it is interesting to note that the health of the average American was better then than it is now. Coincidence?

To select the dishes to present in this book, I did something rather unusual. In an effort to present the best of the American culinary culture, I will not only take you into the American homes where our national cuisine was born, but we will also venture into the aforementioned cafés, diners, truck stops, and roadside eateries where the current resurgence in American food is now taking place. You will find a virtual cornucopia of culinary delights, the blending of old and new, a mixing of traditional and unconventional—all with one tasty goal in mind: the celebration of American food!

Our foray into the tastes of America will begin probably the same way most of us remember eating our first nibble of American food—with something **From the Oven**. In the section called From the Oven, I will share with you some incredible baked delights. Of course there will be a virtual plethora of biscuits. Whether it be a Sunday family dinner or a lunch sitting at the counter of a diner, biscuits have always been a part of the American food scene. As you will soon learn, when it comes to Americana, there is a lot more to biscuits than the tried-and-true buttermilk biscuit.

Breads have always been a part of the American food landscape—and for good reason: they taste good. Of course during the chilly autumn months and the cold winter months, homemade breads were also a way to heat the house as, in the days of yore, many breads were made in an open hearth. As we look at breads, I will delve into some of the classics, and since artisan breads are very popular in the chic cafés dotting the American highways and byways, you will find a few of those as well. If you happen to love the classic American cornbread, I think you'll be pleasantly surprised with the selection I will be presenting.

Of course, it wouldn't be an American kitchen without muffins! Let's face it, there is nothing quite like a warmed muffin with a cup of coffee or tea to start the day. When you get to the muffins, you might notice something kind of strange for a cookbook celebrating America. There is an English muffin recipe. What?! Well, an English muffin really is an adaptation of the classic American griddle cake! Not only are these fun to make, they're easy too, and yes, I'll even tell you how to get those famous "nooks and crannies."

While it may be true that soups did not originate in America (not many foods really did since we are such a young country), the simple fact of the matter is we may have perfected them. Whether it be in grandma's kitchen, at mom's table, or sitting in a diner, truck stop, or café, there is nothing which warms the heart (and brings on memories) like a bowl or mug of homemade soup. In the section cleverly entitled **By the Bowl**, I will pay homage to a wonderful culinary genre of comfort foods: soups, stews, and chilies. This section will take us all across the American landscape and even feature a stew and chili with beer as one of the main ingredients. If you happen to be a fan of Tomato Soup, I think you will find our recipe to be off the charts (page 63)—it is unlike most tomato soups because it is not creamed and tastes like it just came from the garden!

If you are of a certain age (as I am), you very well remember going into diners and cafés and having the waitress (it always seemed to be waitresses) asking you, "What sides would you like with that?" Sometimes the side dishes were actually better than the main course. In American homes, the side dishes usually took up most of the table. In today's hectic world, many people have overlooked side dishes, but in the section called **On the Side**, I bring them back to yummy life. I think everyone will find at least one of these side dishes brings back some memories, and maybe, just maybe, they will once again become a staple of the American dinner table.

I was at a rather nice diner a few weeks ago in Utah, and I ordered a dinner salad. The waitress brought me a bowl of rabbit food with a side of sludge. There was a time in America when salads were actually something you looked forward to. If you went to any church social on a sunny summer Sunday, you would see at least one table laden with fresh yumminess. All roadside types of eateries had a complete salad section on their menus. Moms (and dads) would always have their favorite types of picnic salads. Sounds like Mayberry, doesn't it? In a way, it was—it was pure Americana. In the section brilliantly titled **From the Garden**, I will bring back some of those memories. Remember those crispy fresh coleslaws at the diners? Yep, they're here! How about the colorful carrot salad sold in many delis with that rather interesting dressing and little orbs of sweetness (raisins)? Yep, it's here (including the dressing). We will even venture to the American paradise known as Hawaii and bring you their version of the classic salad known as ambrosia!

Long before anyone reading this book was born (about 1892), many roadside types of eateries had what they called a "blue plate special." Though the history of the "blue plate special" can be argued, what we do know for certain is that it was an entrée (main course) served with two side dishes for one low price. It was usually the special of the house and changed daily. Was it really served on blue plates? At first, yes: a blue metal plate which was divided into three sections. Blue plate specials have become a mainstay at diners and cafés; though they may no longer be the most affordable item on the menu, they are still downright delicious, and in most cases, they still feature classic American fare. In the section called **Blue Plate Specials**, I will dive mouth-first into the most famous of these dishes. You will have your fill of chops, meatloaves (including an adaptation of the legendary

Paul Pruhomme's Cajun Meatloaf which is simply unreal), and yes, there will be quite a variety of fried chicken dishes from all over America, including one made with Coca-Cola® (page 172)!

"You want some gravy?" This was always a common question at most American dinner tables. At most diners throughout America, they didn't bother to ask. You either got gravy over the course you ordered, or you got a little cup of gravy on the side. It's America! We love our gravies. There is just something about this liquefied fat (which most gravies are) that we love. They taste good! They feel good in the mouth! Yes, I want gravy! As an added bonus to this celebration of America and her food, I have added a special section called . . . **America's Gravies!** In this section, I will share with you the favorite gravies of the diners, cafés, and truck stops of America. I have no doubt you will find one of your favorites here, including a real Sausage Gravy (page 221) to drape over some Buttermilk Biscuits (page 8)—now this is a truly American breakfast! Also of note in this section is the famed Tomato Gravy (page 222). This gravy used to be served over meatloaves in many diners, and as we were perfecting the recipe, I realized something. It tastes exactly like Campbell's® Tomato Soup (minus the chemicals and sludge). Maybe I shouldn't admit this, but I ate a bowl of this stuff!

When I was a kid, there were two things I always looked forward to. One was visiting my grandmother and rushing into her pantry where she always kept her fresh-baked goods. The second was the waitress at a diner or café coming to the table and saying with a smile (always with a smile), "Are we ready for dessert?" Just the word "dessert" seems to add a few inches to my waistline, but in my way of thinking, you only live once, so go ahead and have two slices!

Whereas the French and Italians may have perfected the chic and fancy dessert, here in America we have perfected the delicious dessert. Whether it be a freshly baked cake, a pie cooling on the windowsill, or one of our always tempting dessert breads, the American dessert is always the best way to end a meal (or eat as a midnight snack, midday snack, midmorning snack—you get the idea). For the most part, the art of making true American desserts has gone the way of the dodo bird. A perfect example of this is the fact that most Americans have no idea that real brownies do not come out of a box! I will venture to rectify this problem in our section called **All-American Desserts** and even share with you the recipe for the real, true brownie—made with real cocoa. No box! Never a box! One thing you may notice about this section is that we feature a lot of pies. Though pies are not an American creation, they are a true American dessert staple. For all of my pies, whether fruit or cream, I always use the same crust because the simple fact of the matter is: a bad crust can ruin any good pie. The crust I always use, which can be found on page 276, is very simple and French in origin (its actual name is pâte brisée). It is a simple butter crust, but if you're from the South, yes, you can use lard.

When it comes to true American desserts, one does not look at fat or calories. It is for this reason you will notice that all authentic American dessert recipes will use cream, butter, lard, buttermilk, etc. There is nothing wrong with these ingredients. They are all natural, and unlike the processed "stuff" sold in markets, they contain no chemicals or words you cannot pronounce. If you decide to substitute "fat-free" stuff or processed stuff in any of these recipes, don't blame me if the result looks like an escapee from a DOW Chemical plant. When it comes to desserts (or any food really), remember the words of the legendary Julia Child: "Everything in moderation."

Enough words, and now let's get into the kitchen. Let us all celebrate this wondrous nation we call the United States of America and the food we have all come to love, cherish, and remember. Let us become one nation sitting at one table with one goal in mind . . . getting full!

From the Oven

Biscuits, Breads, and Muffins

Angel Biscuits

(Makes 24, depending on size)

When it comes to biscuits, there is an adage that goes, "When is a biscuit not a biscuit?" The answer has always been, "When you're in England because a biscuit there is a cookie." Though this is indeed true, there is another answer, and that answer is . . . when it is an Angel Biscuit!

Why is an Angel Biscuit different from a regular biscuit? Because it is one of the few American biscuits that is made with yeast, and this is also one of the reasons these tasty morsels of dough have the name "angel." The yeast gives these biscuits a rise, thus they are a little more airy or "angel-like."

Many times when you are making biscuits, you are dealing with a rather stiff dough. This is not the case with Angel Biscuits. Matter of fact, quite the opposite is true. This dough is a wet dough, meaning it can be a little messy to make, but sometimes messy can also be fun. You may notice from the ingredients that Angel Biscuits contain both shortening and butter. Yes, these are indeed rather rich, but just wait until the first one meets your mouth!

Ingredients

4 cups flour
¼ cup sugar
1 Tbs. baking powder
1 tsp. baking soda
2 tsp. yeast
2 Tbs. red wine vinegar
2¼ cups milk
1 cup shortening
½ cup butter

Steps

1. In a large bowl, whisk the flour, sugar, baking powder, baking soda, and yeast.
2. In a small bowl, whisk the red wine vinegar and milk. Set the mixture aside 5 minutes for it to curdle.
3. Add the shortening to the flour mixture and, using a pastry blender (or your fingertips), cut the shortening and butter into the flour until it becomes crumbly.

4. Stir the curdled milk into the dough and keep stirring vigorously until it is well blended.

5. Place the dough onto a floured surface and knead for 5 minutes. Have extra flour handy to dust your hands while kneading as the dough is very moist.

6. Re-flour the surface and roll the dough out to a thickness of about ½ inch.

7. Using a 2-inch round cookie- or biscuit cutter, cut out the biscuits.

8. Place the biscuits on a parchment paper–lined baking sheet and let rise 30 minutes.

9. Preheat your oven to 425°F.

10. Place into the oven and bake 20 minutes or until golden.

11. Remove from the oven and let the Angel Biscuits cool on a rack.

Baking Powder Biscuits

(Makes 8, depending on size)

When it comes to truly American biscuits, there may not be a more fitting biscuit than the tried-and-true Baking Powder Biscuit. These biscuits have been around since the beginning of America and were one of the favorite food items carried around by soldiers on both sides during the Civil War.

So, what is baking powder? If you want a scientific answer, buy a science book! Foodwise, it is a simple combination of bicarbonate and a weak acid compound. It is used in biscuits (and breads known as quick breads) as a replacement for yeast. What baking powder does is simple: it increases the volume of the product using heat (baking) and makes the item lighter (edible).

There is a difference between baking powder and baking soda, although baking powder does contain baking soda. Confused? Don't worry about it and just enjoy these biscuits!

Ingredients

2½ cups flour
2 Tbs. baking powder
2 tsp. salt
⅓ cup lard (Yes, you can use shortening, but the texture will be different.)
1½ cups milk

Steps

1. Preheat your oven to 450°F. Line a baking sheet with parchment paper or a silicone baking sheet.

2. In a large bowl, whisk the flour, baking powder, and salt.

3. Add the lard and, with a pastry blender or your fingertips, cut the lard into the flour until it is crumbly.

4. Stir in the milk until you have a dough.

5. Place the dough on a floured surface and knead about 3 minutes.

6. Re-flour your surface and roll the dough out to ½-inch thickness.

7. Using a 2-inch round cookie- or biscuit cutter, cut out the biscuits.
8. Place the biscuits on the prepared baking sheet.
9. Place into the oven and bake 15 minutes or until golden.
10. Remove from the oven and let the biscuits cool on a wire rack.

Beer Biscuits

(Makes 8, depending on size)

Yes, you can have your beer and eat it too! To prove this, I give you biscuits made with beer. Beer is actually one of the oldest known adult beverages made in America (albeit not originating here), so it only makes sense that somewhere down the historic line, someone combined it with some flour to make a biscuit—and for this, we should all be grateful!

A little factoid regarding beer: if beer were created today, it would be considered a "health food" due to the ingredients which make beer. The ingredients needed to make beer, aside from the water, being the hops, grains, etc., are oftentimes some of the same ingredients used to make . . . biscuits! This indeed is a perfect culinary marriage.

On a serious note: Since beer does contain alcohol, you do not want to serve these to anyone who may suffer from an alcohol-related illness. On the other hand, this is a great way to get kids to eat biscuits! Beer Biscuits are one of my favorite biscuits to serve with any type of stew as the texture of the biscuit is perfect for soaking up all that yummy goodness.

Ingredients

2 cups flour
3 tsp. baking powder
1 tsp. salt
¼ cup lard (yes, you can use shortening but the texture will be different)
¾ cup beer (any variety)

Steps

1. Preheat your oven to 450°F. Line a baking sheet with parchment paper or a silicone baking sheet.
2. In a large bowl, whisk the flour, baking powder, and salt.
3. Add the lard and, with a pastry blender or your fingertips, cut the lard into the flour until it is crumbly.
4. Stir in the beer until you have a dough.
5. Place the dough on a floured surface and knead about 3 minutes.
6. Re-flour the surface and roll the dough out to about ½-inch thickness.
7. Using a 2-inch round cookie- or biscuit cutter, cut out the biscuits.

8. Place the biscuits onto the prepared baking sheet.

9. Place into the oven and bake 15 minutes or until golden.

10. Remove from the oven and let cool on a wire rack.

Buttermilk Biscuits

(Makes 12, depending on size)

Earlier in this section on biscuits, I told you about how Baking Powder Biscuits (page 4) are one of the oldest American biscuits. Well . . . Buttermilk Biscuits are one of the most popular! A couple of generations ago, Buttermilk Biscuits were made for almost every meal in certain parts of America. Now, though they are still rather popular, people have a tendency to buy them at fast-food chicken places. Trust me, those pre-baked biscuits are nothing like the real deal!

So, what is buttermilk? Well, there are two types. There is "traditional" buttermilk, which is simply the liquid leftover after churning butter from cream. This was at one time the most popular form of buttermilk and needed no refrigeration. "Traditional" buttermilk is now almost impossible to find at the market. Then there is "cultured" buttermilk— this is cow's milk which has been fortified with a lactic acid bacteria. It is "cultured" buttermilk that you will find at the supermarkets.

What makes Buttermilk Biscuits so special, aside from the tartness of the buttermilk, is the natural chemical reaction between the acidity of the buttermilk and the baking powder and baking soda. This is what creates that unbelievable texture and flavor of real homemade Buttermilk Biscuits.

Ingredients
2 cups flour
2½ tsp. baking powder
½ tsp. baking soda
1 tsp. salt
2 Tbs. lard
1 cup buttermilk

Steps
1. Preheat your oven to 450°F. Line a baking sheet with parchment paper or a silicone baking sheet.
2. In a large bowl, whisk the flour, baking powder, baking soda, and salt.
3. Add the lard and with a pastry blender or your fingertips, cut the lard into the flour until it is crumbly.
4. Stir in the buttermilk to form a dough.
5. Place the dough onto a floured surface and knead about 2 minutes.

6. Re-flour the surface and roll the dough out to ½-inch thickness.
7. Using a 2-inch round cookie- or biscuit cutter, cut out the biscuits.
8. Place the biscuits on the prepared baking sheet.
9. Place into the oven and bake 15 minutes or until golden.
10. Remove from the oven and let cool on a wire rack.

Corn Pone

(Makes 4 pieces)

Chances are you have heard of Corn Pone. Though it is a food item, the words "corn pone" are usually used in a derogatory way to describe someone of Southern heritage, much like the word "hick" or "hillbilly." Factually, Corn Pone is a form of cornbread, but what makes it different is the lack of a simple ingredient. Corn Pone, as opposed to cornbread, does not feature eggs.

For those of a literate persuasion, you might know of Corn Pone from the writings of Mark Twain. Mr. Twain was a big fan of Corn Pone and was known to make it whenever he was privy to the ingredients. When you first make Corn Pone, you might think you are doing something wrong. It is a dough instead of a batter, and it is very thick. So thick that you actually hand-form the dough.

Authentic Corn Pone was always made in a cast iron skillet. Nowadays, Corn Pone is usually baked in a very hot oven on a baking sheet. If you really want a great Southern breakfast, make some Corn Pone and top it with some sweet butter and maple syrup.

Ingredients

1 cup yellow cornmeal
1 tsp. baking powder
½ tsp. salt
2 Tbs. melted butter
½ cup milk

Steps

1. Preheat your oven to 425°F. Line a baking sheet with parchment paper or a silicone baking sheet.
2. In a medium bowl, whisk the cornmeal, baking powder, and salt.
3. Stir in the melted butter and milk to form a stiff dough.
4. Divide the dough into 4 oval cakes.
5. Place the Corn Pone on the prepared baking sheet.
6. Place into the oven and bake 30 minutes.
7. Remove from the oven and let cool slightly before serving.

Cream Biscuits

(Makes 12, depending on size)

Aside from boiling water, this may very well be the easiest recipe you will ever find. It contains only two ingredients. Trust me, you can't mess this recipe up (unless you can't read the oven dial). These are Cream Biscuits, and all you need are some flour and some cream. Yep, that's it!

Now you might be saying to yourself, "These can't work." At first glance, you might be right. When you think about it, however, you are dead wrong. Let me explain. Liquid and flour cannot give you a biscuit. They can give you dough rocks but not biscuits. You need fat. Aha! This is where the cream comes in as it is, essentially, a liquid fat. By the way, don't even think of substituting anything for the cream. The cream is essential for these biscuits to be edible.

As you might surmise from looking at this recipe, your dough is going to be much different than a typical biscuit. It will be very stiff, and it is not the easiest dough to roll out. Just take your time, and everything will turn out just wonderful.

Ingredients

2 cups flour
1¼ cups heavy cream

Steps

1. Preheat your oven to 450°F. Line a baking sheet with parchment paper or a silicone baking sheet.
2. In a large bowl, stir the flour and heavy cream to form a dough.
3. Place the dough on a floured surface and knead until it comes together.
4. Re-flour the surface and roll the dough out to ½-inch thickness.
5. Using a 2-inch round cookie- or biscuit cutter, cut out the biscuits.
6. Place the biscuits onto the prepared baking sheet.
7. Place into the oven and bake 12 minutes or until golden.
8. Remove from the oven and let cool on a rack.

Ham and Cheese Biscuits

(Makes 12, depending on size)

These biscuits are so addictive, they should have a wing at the Betty Ford Clinic dedicated just to them. Just imagine your mouth going around a wonderfully flaky biscuit oozing with melted Monterey Jack cheese and laden with ham. Serve these with a fried egg or two and a cup of hot coffee, and you have one incredible breakfast!

Ham and Cheese Biscuits are a Southern favorite, but no one really knows how they came about. One can only surmise that some brilliant Southern cook was simply making some biscuits, noticed there was some extra cheese and ham hanging around, and just plopped them into the dough. Eh, makes sense to me.

Aside from the ham and cheese, what really sets these biscuits apart is the perfect blending of flour and cornmeal—which right there tells you these are Southern. So what happens here is you get the flaky biscuit texture you're used to, along with the added slight crunch of the cornmeal. This, my friends, is perfection.

Ingredients

1⅔ cups flour
⅓ cup yellow cornmeal
1 Tbs. baking powder
1 Tbs. sugar
¼ tsp. salt
¼ cup butter, chilled
½ cup shredded Monterey Jack cheese
½ cup cooked minced ham
1 green onion, minced
¾ cup milk

Steps

1. Preheat your oven to 425°F. Line a baking sheet with parchment paper or a silicone baking sheet.
2. In a large bowl, whisk the flour, cornmeal, baking powder, sugar, and salt.
3. Add the butter and, using a pastry blender or your fingertips, cut the butter into the flour until it is crumbly.
4. Stir in the cheese, ham, onion, and milk until you have a dough.
5. Place the dough on a floured surface and knead until the dough comes together.

6. Re-flour the surface and roll the dough out to ¾-inch thickness.

7. Using a 2-inch round cookie- or biscuit cutter, cut out the biscuits.

8. Place the biscuits on the prepared baking sheet.

9. Place into the oven and bake 13 minutes or until golden.

10. Remove from the oven and cool on a wire rack.

··· **Note** ···

When you first begin to knead the dough, it will be very stiff. This is natural; you've done nothing wrong. As these biscuits bake, the moisture from both the ham and the cheese will evolve within the dough to create a perfect texture.

Hominy Biscuits

(Makes 12, depending on size)

The first time I ever had hominy, I looked at it and said, "No way." My mother said, "It's corn; eat it!" Well, Mom, you were only sorta right, but since you weren't from the South, you're to be forgiven. On this subject, hominy is not corn as most people away from the South know corn. It is maize, and yes, there is a botanical difference.

So, now that we know corn is maize and a member of the corn family, what really is hominy? Well . . . hominy actually goes back to before the days of Christ, but for the sake of our fun in the kitchen, we'll center on the American hominy. For this treat, we can actually thank the American Indians as they were making hominy before there was an America. Hominy is a dried maize which has been treated with an alkali solution which, yes, does contain lye.

For the sake of fairness, I should say here that I cannot stand hominy from the can, but I do indeed like it when used in Hominy Biscuits. What the hominy does in these slightly sweet biscuits is give them a different texture. With every bite, you get the slight softness of the hominy. It's different, and it's enjoyable. Just remember to drain and rinse the hominy before you add them to the dough.

Ingredients

1½ Tbs. yeast
⅓ cup warm water
¼ cup honey
1 cup hominy, drained and rinsed (yes, the canned variety)
½ cup butter, softened
2 cups flour

Steps

1. Line a baking sheet with parchment paper or a silicone baking sheet.
2. In a small bowl, whisk the yeast, water, and honey. Set the bowl aside 5 minutes for the yeast to proof (foam).
3. In a large bowl, stir together the proofed yeast mixture, hominy, butter, and flour until you have a dough.
4. Place the dough on a floured surface and knead 5 minutes.
5. Place the dough back into the bowl, cover, and let rise 1 hour.

6. Place the dough onto a floured surface and knead a few minutes to release the air from its rising.

7. Roll the dough into a rectangle (size doesn't matter). Fold the dough over onto itself and roll it out again. Do this four times.

8. When rolling the dough the fourth time, roll it to ½-inch thickness.

9. Using a 2-inch round cookie- or biscuit cutter, cut out the biscuits.

10. Place the biscuits onto the prepared baking sheet.

11. Let the biscuits rest 30 minutes.

12. Meanwhile, preheat your oven to 350°F.

13. Place the Hominy Biscuits in the oven and bake 20 minutes or until golden.

14. Remove from the oven and let cool on a wire rack.

··· **Note** ···

When you first go to knead this dough, it will feel stiff (dry). It will become moister as you knead it since the hominy does contain quite a bit of moisture.

Hoe Cakes

(Serving amount depends on size)

Now that you have read the title, I will wait until your juvenile humor abates.

Okay, now let's get to history! The origins of Hoe Cakes actually go way back before there was an America (as we know it). According to food historians, Hoe Cakes, albeit it under a different name, were originated by the American Indians. They became known as Hoe Cakes when they were being made by slaves in the south. According to legend, the slaves would make a cornmeal mixture and cook it over an open fire on the blades of a garden hoe. Thus the name, Hoe Cakes.

There are those who will claim that Hoe Cakes are the same as Johnnycakes. This is not true. There are some resemblances, but they are in fact two different dishes. This recipe calls for the inclusion of bacon fat. There is a belief that the original Hoe Cakes did not use bacon fat but lard. This may be true for the American Indian version, but the fact of the matter is, the slaves did indeed use bacon fat.

By the way, you don't need to cook these in your backyard with a garden hoe. A frying pan or skillet will work just fine.

Ingredients

¼ cup bacon fat, divided
2 cups cornmeal
1 cup flour
2 tsp. baking powder
1 tsp. salt
2 Tbs. sugar
1 cup milk

Steps

1. In a medium skillet over medium heat, melt (liquefy) 3 tablespoons of the bacon fat.
2. In a medium bowl, whisk the cornmeal, flour, baking powder, salt, and sugar.
3. Stir in the remaining bacon fat and milk to form a stiff batter.
4. Drop batter by the tablespoon into the skillet with hot bacon fat and fry for about 3 minutes.
5. Turn the Hoe Cakes over and fry an additional 3 minutes.
6. Remove the Hoe Cakes to a paper towel–lined plate and serve.

Potato Biscuits

(Makes 6, depending on size)

Simply put, Potato Biscuits are some of the best biscuits ever created. These are so delicate that they will literally melt in your mouth. There is, however, a bad side to these biscuits. They must be eaten within a few hours after they bake as time is not their best friend. I don't really think this will be a problem as, once you eat one, you will be hooked.

Potato biscuits were created in America due to potatoes being very cheap, and they were a great way to use leftover mashed potatoes. During the time of the biscuit's greatest popularity, you never let any food go to waste—you just made biscuits!

If you're used to making biscuits but have never tried these, then just wait until you feel this dough. It is heavenly. It is so soft that it cannot be rolled out. You have to pat it out with floured hands. Yes, food can be fun. These are one of my favorite biscuits to serve with any variety of fried chicken.

Ingredients

1 cup flour
3 Tsp. baking powder
1 tsp. salt
2 Tbs. rendered bacon fat
1 cup mashed potatoes
½ cup milk

Steps

1. Preheat your oven to 400°F. Line a baking sheet with parchment paper or a silicone baking sheet.
2. In a medium bowl, whisk the flour, baking powder, and salt.
3. Stir in the bacon fat and the mashed potatoes until the mixture is moistened.
4. Slowly stir in the milk to form a dough.
5. Place the dough onto a floured surface and, with floured hands, pat the dough into a ½-inch thick disc.
6. Using a 2-inch round cookie- or biscuit cutter, cut out the biscuits.
7. Place the biscuits onto the prepared baking sheet.
8. Place into the oven and bake 15 minutes.
9. Remove from the oven and let cool on a wire rack.

Sweet Potato Biscuits

(Makes 12, depending on size)

When is a potato not a potato? When it is a sweet potato. Botanically speaking, a common potato and a sweet potato are not really related. Their only similarity is the fact that they are both tuberous roots. If you want to pick out the sweetest sweet potatoes, cut them open. The ones with the most vibrant flesh are the sweetest . . . and this concludes today's Sweet Potato 101 lesson.

So, are sweet potatoes and yams the same edible creature? No, they are not. Though they are often referred to interchangeably in many parts of the world, they are different, and in the United States, it is actually illegal to misrepresent them. Fact: Markets must correctly label sweet potatoes and/or yams or face a fine from the United States Department of Agriculture.

Sweet potatoes (and yams) came to America via the slave trade. Both of these tubers were very popular in Africa, and the slaves used them in many dishes when they started to cook on the plantations. No one actually knows when Sweet Potato Biscuits were first made in America, but we do know they were quite popular during the plantation days and all the way through the Great Depression.

By the way, you can indeed use yams to make these biscuits.

Ingredients

4 cups flour
2 Tbs. baking powder
2 tsp. salt
1 cup butter, chilled and diced
1 cup mashed sweet potatoes
1 cup buttermilk

Steps

1. Preheat your oven to 425°F. Line a baking sheet with parchment paper or a silicone baking sheet.

2. In a large bowl, whisk the flour, baking powder, and salt.

3. Add the butter, and using a pastry blender or your fingertips, cut the butter into the flour until it is crumbly.

4. In a medium bowl, stir the mashed sweet potatoes and buttermilk until smooth.
5. Stir the sweet potato mixture into the flour mixture to form a dough.
6. Place the dough onto a floured surface and knead 2 minutes.
7. Re-flour the surface and roll the dough out to ½-inch thickness.
8. Using a 2-inch round cookie- or biscuit cutter, cut out the biscuits.
9. Place the biscuits onto the prepared baking sheet.
10. Place into the oven and bake 15 minutes or until golden.
11. Remove from the oven and let cool on a wire rack.

Chorizo Upside-Down Cornbread

(Makes one 8- or 9-inch round cornbread)

If you are of the thought that anything made in an American kitchen is considered American food, then cornbread is a native dish. Fact of the matter is, though, cornbread had been around for centuries before America was colonized and was a favorite food staple of the natives. Also of note is the fact that areas of Mexico and South America are also in the mix when it comes to creating cornbread.

Chorizo Upside-Down Cornbread is a classic presentation from the great American Southwest. I not only love to eat this cornbread, I also love to make it. This is really quite a simple dish. You make the Jalapeño Cornbread batter (page 30), and you spoon it over the chorizo mixture I give you here. This is pretty much a foolproof dish!

You can also make Chorizo Upside-Down Cornbread a complete meal by adding one simple touch. Once you have cut the cornbread into serving pieces, top it with enchilada sauce, and a dollop of sour cream. YUM!

Ingredients

1 pound bulk chorizo
1 yellow onion, chopped
1 red bell pepper, diced
1 cup grated Monterey Jack cheese
1 recipe of Jalapeño Cornbread batter (page 30)

Steps

1. Preheat your oven to 400°F.

2. In a large oven-safe skillet over medium heat, add the chorizo, onion, and red bell pepper and cook 10 minutes.

3. Remove and discard any rendered fat.

4. Layer the cheese atop the chorizo mixture.
5. Spoon the Jalapeño Cornbread batter over the cheese and even out.
6. Place into the oven and bake 20 minutes.
7. Remove from the oven and let cool slightly before serving.

Cinnamon Bread

(Makes 2 loaves)

If you have never had a breakfast of toasted homemade Cinnamon Bread and piping hot chocolate, you have not lived! Many areas of America have their own version of Cinnamon Bread, and they are all delicious. This particular version comes from the Midwest, and the bread dough also features oatmeal. This leads to not only a great texture but also a hefty dose of fiber . . . and that's a good thing!

This is a yeast bread, so it will take some time before you can start pigging-out on it. Cinnamon Bread needs a couple of rising periods to attain its perfect texture. This is also a recipe you can play with a little. If you want more cinnamon, add more. You can also add raisins to the dough without having to change any of the baking instructions.

This recipe does make two loaves, but the good thing is that Cinnamon Bread freezes quite well. Once the loaves are completely cooled, wrap them in some waxed paper, then foil, and freeze.

Ingredients

1 cup milk
1 Tbs. butter, softened
1 cup warm water
2½ tsp. yeast
1 Tbs. honey
1 Tbs. salt
1 Tbs. vanilla
1 cup brown sugar, divided
2 eggs, beaten
2 cups oatmeal
5½ cups flour, divided
1 Tbs. ground cinnamon
2 Tbs. melted butter

Steps

1. In a small saucepan over medium heat, combine the milk and butter just until it comes to a simmer.

2. In a large bowl, whisk the warm water, yeast, and honey. Let the yeast mixture sit 5 minutes to proof (foam).

3. Into the hot milk, stir salt, vanilla, and ¼ cup of the brown sugar. Remove the milk from the heat and let cool slightly.

4. Stir the milk mixture into the proofed yeast.

5. Stir in the eggs and oatmeal until well blended.

6. Stir in 3 cups of the flour to form a wet dough.

7. Place the dough on a floured surface and knead the remaining 2½ cups flour into the dough.

8. Place the dough back into the bowl, cover, and let rise 2 hours.

9. Remove the dough from the bowl and divide in half.

10. On a floured surface, roll each portion of dough into a rectangle, about 13x8 inches.

11. In a small bowl, stir together the remaining brown sugar and cinnamon.

12. Sprinkle the cinnamon-sugar mixture over the dough.

13. Roll the dough up (jellyroll fashion), making sure to pinch the sides to seal the dough.

14. Line the bottom of two 9x5-inch loaf pans with parchment paper. Place one piece of dough into each pan and let rise 60 minutes.

15. Preheat your oven to 400°F.

16. Place the loaves into the oven and bake 10 minutes.

17. Lower the heat to 350°F and bake 30 minutes.

18. Remove the loaves from the oven and brush the tops with the melted butter.

19. Remove the loaves from the pan and let cool on a wire rack.

Creamy Cornbread

(Makes one 9-inch cornbread)

When it comes to cornbread, you have two kinds: Southern cornbread and then all the rest. How can you tell if a cornbread is Southern in origin? It will have either rendered bacon- or sausage fat in the batter. Why? Well, that is a good question, and the reason may be as simple as: Southerners will cook their cornbread in a cast iron pan—the same pan they fried their bacon or sausage in, so instead of cleaning it out, they just bake the cornbread in it!

Creamy Cornbread is an interesting cornbread because it is prepared unlike any other cornbread. Creamy Cornbread actually starts off as a polenta. Once you delve into the recipe, you'll see what I am talking about.

There are many cornbread recipes from around the country, which feature certain dairy products. Matter of fact, two of the most common ingredients in many cornbread recipes are buttermilk and/or sour cream. This cornbread contains neither of these. It does, interestingly enough, contain heavy cream.

Ingredients

3 cups yellow cornmeal
2 tsp. salt
1 Tbs. rendered bacon fat
1¼ cups boiling water
2 eggs
1 cup heavy cream
2 tsp. baking powder

Steps

1. Preheat your oven to 400°F and place a 10-inch cake pan, lined with parchment paper, in the oven while it is preheating.

2. In a large bowl, whisk the cornmeal and salt.

3. Stir in the bacon fat and boiling water and keep stirring until the cornmeal is completely moistened. The mixture will be quite thick.

4. Stir in the eggs, heavy cream, and baking powder. Once all combined, give it a few very vigorous stirs.

5. Spoon the mixture into the hot pan and even out.
6. Place back into the oven and bake 40 minutes.
7. Remove from the oven and let the cornbread cool in the pan 10 minutes.
8. Remove from the pan and cool on a wire rack.

Hamburger Buns

(Makes 4 large buns)

Who doesn't love a perfectly grilled or griddled hamburger? There is just something pure Americana about biting into a burger and having the juices drip down your chin. Napkins be damned, a good burger is meant to be messy!

Though the most important part of a good hamburger is quality ground beef, the second most important part is the bun. Yes, the bun! If you have a crappy bun, everything falls apart, or it turns mushy—and the whole joy of eating the burger is taken away. The fact is, I have never seen one of those buns sold in bags hold up to a real burger. This will change when you begin to make your own!

A real hamburger bun is sort of an adaptation of a brioche bread. It is a rather wet dough and can get a little messy to make, but sometimes messy can be fun—and it is always delicious. This recipe is quite simple to make, and once you try these buns, you'll never use store-bought again.

Ingredients

½ cup warm water
1 Tbs. butter, softened
1 egg
2 cups flour
¼ cup sugar
3 tsp. salt
2 tsp. yeast
1 Tbs. melted butter

Steps

1. Place all the ingredients, except the melted butter, into a large bowl and vigorously stir until you have a dough. It will be sticky; no need to knead at this point.
2. Cover the bowl and let the dough rise 2 hours.
3. Punch down the dough (yes, put your fist into it), then remove it to a floured surface, and knead about 5 minutes.
4. Divide the dough into four equal portions.
5. Using floured hands, shape the dough into buns, and place on a baking sheet lined with parchment paper or a silicone baking sheet.

6. Let the buns rise 1 hour.
7. Preheat your oven to 375°F.
8. Brush the tops of the buns with the melted butter.
9. Place into the oven and bake 18–20 minutes (depending on the size of the bun).
10. Remove from the oven and let cool on a wire rack until ready to serve.

--- · · · **Note** · · · ---

During the kneading process, you'll want to have some flour standing by to make things a little easier. Keep your hands and the counter top well-floured, and you'll have no problems.

Herb Cottage Bread

(Makes 1 loaf)

This is one of my favorite breads of all time. It is a soft-crust bread with an angelic texture. The flavors of the combined herbs are heavenly, and just wait until you get a drift of the aroma when it wafts through your humble abode.

Adding cheese to bread is a very American thing to do. Most of our cheese bread varieties originated in the Northwest of the United States. Herb Cottage Bread, however, was originated in the Northeast, yet the exact location is unknown. Which cheese will we be using for this bread? Cottage cheese—and for the best results, you will want to use a small curd cottage cheese.

Whenever I make this bread (which is very often), I always use fresh herbs simply because my herb garden is right outside my kitchen. You can use dried herbs as well, but since dried herbs have a more condensed flavor, you might want to slightly lower the amounts.

Ingredients

1 Tbs. honey
2½ tsp. yeast
½ cup warm water
2½ cups flour
1 cup small curd cottage cheese, drained
1 egg, beaten
2 scallions (green onions), minced
1 Tbs. sugar
1 tsp. salt
1 Tbs. minced oregano
1 Tbs. minced basil
1 Tbs. minced rosemary
2 Tbs. melted butter

Steps

1. In a small bowl, whisk the honey, yeast, and water. Set the mixture aside to proof (foam).

2. In a large bowl, stir the flour, cottage cheese, egg, scallions, sugar, salt, herbs, and proofed yeast.

3. Cover the bowl and let rise 2 hours.

4. Stir the dough down in the bowl (it is too moist to knead).

5. Line the bottom of a 9x5-inch loaf pan with parchment paper.

6. Spoon the dough into the prepared loaf pan and let it rest 30 minutes.

7. Preheat your oven to 350°F.

8. Place the bread into the oven and bake 10 minutes.

9. Remove the bread from the oven and brush the top with the melted butter.

10. Place the bread back into the oven and bake 35 minutes.

11. Remove the bread from the oven and let cool in the pan 10 minutes.

12. Remove the bread from the pan and let cool on a wire rack.

Jalapeño Cornbread

(Makes one 9-inch cornbread)

Have you ever heard the adage "Everything is bigger in Texas?" That is kind of true, and it includes their cornbread. Jalapeño Cornbread is a Texas tradition, albeit came to the Lone Star State via their neighbors from the south (Mexico). This is also a very simple cornbread to make.

You can make this cornbread two ways: hot or not-so-hot. If you want to make it hot, once you remove the stem end from the jalapeño peppers, mince them with their seeds and all. If you want to make it not-so-hot, once you remove the stem, slice the peppers down the middle and remove the seeds and membrane (the white pithy stuff). Most of the heat in peppers is in the seeds and membrane.

This cornbread is not a Southern texture type of cornbread (which is usually on the dry side). This is a rather moist cornbread, and it actually features corn—not just cornmeal. With this being a Texas type of cornbread, it only makes sense that it goes perfectly with a big bowl of Texas Chili (page 88).

Ingredients

3 Tbs. corn oil
1 cup yellow cornmeal
1 cup flour
2 Tbs. honey
1 Tbs. baking powder
1 tsp. salt
1 cup buttermilk
1 cup Creamed Corn (page 104)
3 eggs, beaten
4 jalapeño peppers, minced
4 scallions (green onions), minced
2 Tbs. sour cream
¼ cup melted butter

Steps

1. Preheat your oven to 400°F. Line the bottom of a 9-inch cake pan with parchment paper.

2. In a large bowl, combine all of the ingredients and vigorously stir until you have a batter.

3. Spoon the batter into the prepared cake pan.

4. Place into the oven and bake 30 minutes.

5. Remove from the oven and let the Jalapeño Cornbread cool in the pan 10 minutes.

6. Remove the Jalapeño Cornbread from the pan and let cool on a wire rack.

Oat Bread

(Makes 1 loaf)

You can go any into a store in any state and buy a package of oat bread. You can go into any bakery in any state and buy a loaf of oat bread. The fact of the matter is you have never really tasted and/or enjoyed oat bread until you have made it yourself.

I first tasted this version of Oat Bread a few decades ago while traveling in the Northeast. It is the best Oat Bread I have ever eaten, and unlike many other oat breads, with this one, you can actually taste the nuttiness of the oats.

When I make this Oat Bread, I always use instant oats. There is nothing wrong with them. They simply cook faster because they have been steamed before they were dried. The one thing you do want to remember is to let the oats totally cool before you begin to knead the bread. Speaking of kneading this bread, this is a rather sticky dough, so it can get a little messy during the kneading process.

Ingredients

1 cup boiling water
1 cup oats
1 Tbs. butter
2 tsp. yeast
¼ cup warm water
1 Tbs. sugar
¼ cup brown sugar
2 cups flour, divided
1 tsp. salt

Steps

1. In a large bowl, stir the boiling water, oats, and butter. Let the mixture cool.
2. In a small bowl, whisk the yeast, warm water, and both sugars. Set the bowl aside 5 minutes for the yeast to proof (foam).
3. Into the oats, stir the proofed yeast and 1 cup of flour. Cover the bowl and let the dough rise 1 hour.
4. Stir the remaining flour and salt into the bowl. Place the dough onto a floured surface and knead about 5 minutes. Have extra flour on hand as this is a rather wet (messy) dough.

5. Place the dough back into the bowl, cover the bowl, and let the dough rise 1 hour.

6. Line a 9x5-inch loaf pan with parchment paper.

7. Place the dough into the prepared loaf pan and let the dough rise 1 hour.

8. Preheat your oven to 350°F.

9. Place the bread into the oven and bake 45 minutes.

10. Remove the bread from the oven and let it cool in the pan 10 minutes.

11. Remove the bread from the pan and let it cool on a rack.

Onion and Olive Bread

(Makes 1 loaf)

There used to be a time in America when a freshly baked loaf of bread was served at every dinner. Those times have since gone the way of the dodo bird, but unlike the dodo bird, we can bring them back. This bread, a delicious Onion and Olive Bread, was often served at family dinners on the holidays (Thanksgiving, Christmas, etc.). Since it is a yeast bread, it does have a few rising periods, so start the bread about four to five hours before you start the dinner.

To make this dish authentically, you would use pitted black olives. If you don't like black olives, you can use green olives, and I have even used stuffed green olives without removing the pimiento or whatever else it was stuffed with. There really is no need to rinse the olives of their brine unless you want to cut down on salt.

This is a shaped bread. This means is it is not baked in a pan. You shape the bread with your hands and then place it onto the baking sheet (or baking stone). The easiest and cleanest way to hand-shape dough is to keep your hands dusted with flour.

Ingredients

1 Tbs. yeast
1 cup warm water, divided
1 Tbs. honey
4½ cups flour
1 tsp. salt
¼ cup olive oil
¾ cup chopped black olives
1 small red onion, minced
1 Tbs. melted butter

Steps

1. In a small bowl, whisk the yeast, ¼ cup of the warm water, and the honey. Set the bowl aside 5 minutes for the yeast to proof (foam).

2. In a large bowl, whisk the flour and salt.

3. Into the flour, stir the olive oil, olives, and onion.

4. Stir in the proofed yeast and remaining water until a dough is formed.

5. Place the dough on a floured surface and knead 10 minutes (yes, it takes a bit of kneading to get the proper texture for the bread).

6. Place the dough back into the bowl, cover, and let rise 2 hours.

7. Punch the dough down (yes, put your fist into it), and remove it from the bowl onto a floured surface.

8. Shape the dough into a round loaf and let it rise 1 hour.

9. Preheat your oven to 400°F. Line a baking sheet with parchment paper or a silicone baking sheet.

10. Place the bread onto the prepared baking sheet.

11. Place into the oven and bake 45 minutes.

12. Remove the bread from the oven and brush with the melted butter.

13. Place the bread on a wire rack to cool.

Red Pepper and Dill Cornbread

(Makes one 9-inch cornbread)

This cornbread is what is known as a California or West Coast cornbread for the simple reason that it is loaded with freshness—elements which make up the cuisine known as California Cooking. Of course, it is also a great and flavorful cornbread which goes wonderfully well with a nice California wine for a brunch on the patio.

As opposed to many Southern styles of cornbread, Red Pepper and Dill Cornbread features a blended combination of yellow cornmeal and flour. This makes the texture somewhat lighter and less granular. It also gives you a taller cornbread as the dough is lighter and able to rise more while baking.

Though there are many cornbread recipes which call for the inclusion of creamed corn, this one has freshly shucked sweet corn in the batter (and yes, you can substitute good quality organic frozen sweet corn). By using whole corn kernels in this cornbread, each bite will contain little bits of pure and natural flavor.

Ingredients

2 Tbs. olive oil
¼ cup minced sweet red bell pepper
½ tsp. red pepper flakes
1 clove garlic, minced
1¼ cups flour
1 cup yellow cornmeal
1 Tbs. baking powder
1 tsp. baking soda
½ tsp. salt
1 cup buttermilk
1 egg, beaten
1 cup sweet corn kernels
¼ cup minced dill

Steps

1. Preheat your oven to 400°F. Line the bottom of a 9-inch cake pan with parchment paper.

2. In a small pan, heat the olive oil over medium heat. Add the red bell pepper, pepper flakes, and garlic and sauté 3 minutes.

3. In a large bowl, whisk the flour, cornmeal, baking powder, baking soda, and salt.

4. Stir the pepper mixture into the flour.

5. In a medium bowl, whisk the buttermilk, egg, corn, and dill.

6. Stir the buttermilk mixture into the flour mixture until blended.

7. Spoon the batter into the prepared pan.

8. Place into the oven and bake 30 minutes.

9. Remove from the oven and let cool in the pan 10 minutes.

10. Remove from the pan and let cool on a wire rack.

Savory Breadsticks

(Makes 4 large breadsticks)

There was a time in America when breadsticks were one of the most popular bread items you could find. They came in two varieties: soft and hard. Then something happened, and breadsticks virtually disappeared. About twenty or so years ago, thanks to the fast-food eatery known as Olive Garden, breadsticks once again became popular—albeit the Olive Garden version and the real deal are miles apart in flavor and nutrition.

Personally, I absolutely love breadsticks, and this particular version is my favorite—you will find them in my kitchen all the time. They are very simple to make, and you can make the topping however you choose. My choices are always fresh herbs, seasoning, and sometimes grated cheese.

Savory Breadsticks are a soft variety. Because they are formed by hand, you can make them any length or width you like, and the baking time will be about the same. Now, here is an added bonus when you make these. Once they start to get a little stale, you can cut the breadsticks to make some croutons, or as I often do, put them into a food processor and make your own seasoned breadcrumbs!

Ingredients

2 tsp. yeast
1 cup warm water, divided
1 Tbs. sugar
2 cups flour
2 Tbs. cornstarch
2 tsp. salt
1 Tbs. vegetable oil
whatever topping your little heart desires!

Steps

1. In a small bowl, whisk the yeast, ¼ cup warm water, and sugar. Set the bowl aside 5 minutes for the yeast to proof (foam).
2. In a medium bowl, whisk the flour, cornstarch, and salt.
3. Stir in the proofed yeast and remaining ¾ cup water to form a dough.
4. Place the dough on a floured surface and knead 5 minutes.
5. Place the dough back into the bowl, cover, and let rise 1 hour.
6. Place the dough onto a floured surface and divide into 4 pieces.

7. Using your hands, form each piece of dough into a log.

8. Line a baking sheet with parchment paper or a silicone baking sheet.

9. Place the pieces of dough on the prepared baking sheet and let rest 30 minutes (they will rise a little).

10. Brush the breadsticks with vegetable oil and top with whatever herbs or seasoning you like.

11. Place into the oven and bake 15 minutes.

12. Remove from the oven and let the breadsticks cool on a wire rack.

Spanish Cornbread

(Makes one 9-inch cornbread)

Just take a look at the list of the ingredients for this cornbread, and you might say, "Whoa, that cornbread is like a meal in itself!" It is . . . almost. Though this is a Spanish Cornbread, whenever I make it, I think of it along the lines of a stuffed cornbread—and it does indeed make a complete meal when you top a large slice of it with some chili!

Since the cornbread does feature fresh chili peppers, remember the simple rule of peppers: if you want it hot, leave the seeds and the membrane; if you don't, then remove the seeds and the membrane (the white pithy part inside the pepper). It should be noted that jalapeño peppers are not really that hot to begin with.

This is a constructed cornbread. What that means is that you do not simply put the batter into a pan. There are a few steps to putting this cornbread together. They are very simple and take virtually no time at all. This is the perfect cornbread to serve when you are having a dinner featuring Southwest or Texas food.

Ingredients

1 cup yellow cornmeal
1 cup flour
¼ cup sugar
1 Tbs. baking powder
1 tsp. salt
1 egg, beaten
2 scallions (green onions), minced
2 cloves garlic, minced
1 cup milk
1 cup sour cream
½ cup corn oil
6 jalapeño peppers, minced
1½ cups grated cheddar cheese

Steps

1. Preheat your oven to 400°F. Line the bottom of a 9-inch cake pan with parchment paper.

2. In a medium bowl, whisk the cornmeal, flour, sugar, baking powder, and salt.

3. In a large bowl, whisk the egg, scallions, garlic, milk, sour cream, and corn oil.

4. Stir the cornmeal mixture into the milk mixture until you have a batter.

5. Spoon half of the batter into the prepared pan.

6. Over the batter, scatter the jalapeño peppers, and then top with the cheese.

7. Spoon the remaining batter over the cheese and even out.

8. Place into the oven and bake 35–40 minutes or until the top is rich gold in color.

9. Remove the cornbread from the oven and let cool in the pan 10 minutes.

10. Remove the cornbread from the pan and let cool on a wire rack.

Spoon Bread

(Serves 6)

To be totally honest, this isn't a bread at all. Well, it is not a bread as we have all become accustomed to. It really is a pudding or soufflé. Confused? Don't worry about it—it is easy and delicious and totally Southern!

How Spoon Bread came about is anyone's guess. Hell, even the spelling of this dish is anyone's guess. You can find it as "Spoonbread" or "Spoon Bread." We do know it is a classic Southern dish, but we do not know where it originated. There is plenty of proof that American Indians made a dish similar to this; then again, so did many tribes in Africa—so maybe it was brought to the South via the slaves (as were most dishes considered to be Southern). Whatever the facts surrounding this dish are, one thing is for certain: it is delicious!

To make this dish, you will need a large, deep skillet or sauté pan. It must be deep because Spoon Bread rises the same way a soufflé does. If the pan is not deep enough, you will have a mess inside your oven. By the way, if you are the type who likes to use low-fat or non-fat milk instead of whole milk for recipes, do NOT do it with this dish, or you will ruin it.

Ingredients

3 cups whole milk
1¼ cups yellow cornmeal
3 eggs
1 tsp. salt
1¾ tsp. baking powder
¼ cup melted butter

Steps

1. Preheat your oven to 400°F.

2. In a medium pot, bring the milk just to a boil over medium heat.

3. In a slow stream, whisk in the cornmeal and keep whisking until the mixture has thickened; then remove the pot from the heat.

4. Spoon the cornmeal into a mixer with the paddle attachment and beat on high speed for 1 minute.

5. Lower the speed on the mixer to medium and add the eggs, one at a time, beating for a few minutes.

6. Add the salt, baking powder, and melted butter and beat on medium-high speed for 10 minutes—yes, 10 minutes!

7. Oil the bottom and sides of a large, deep skillet or sauté pan.

8. Spoon the batter into the prepared skillet.

9. Place into the oven and bake 25 minutes. Do NOT open the oven door during the baking process.

10. Remove from the oven and serve. The Spoon Bread will deflate as it cools.

Whole Wheat Honey Bread

(Makes 1 loaf)

I suppose if one was to be literal, every bread made with flour from wheat would be a "wheat bread." In the world of food, however, a wheat bread is a bread made from whole wheat, which is usually stone ground and has a darker hue than regular flour, whether bleached or unbleached.

When it comes to homemade breads, the American leader has always been Whole Wheat Bread. There are numerous adaptations of Whole Wheat Breads in cookbooks and online, and while all of them can be rather tasty, for my money, I prefer the simplicity and natural goodness of Whole Wheat Honey Bread.

This is one of the better sandwich-type breads around because the texture of the bread is rather dense, meaning it can handle the ingredients of a sandwich without falling apart. Though it does contain honey, it is not really sweet. The honey is simply used as food for the yeast and quickens the proofing process. It is best to make a bread of this variety one loaf at a time because it does not stand up well to freezing.

Ingredients

1¼ cups warm milk
2 Tbs. honey
2 tsp. yeast
2 Tbs. corn oil
2 tsp. salt
1½ cups flour (all-purpose white flour)
1½ cups whole wheat flour

Steps

1. In a medium bowl, whisk the milk, honey, and yeast. Set the bowl aside 5 minutes for the yeast to proof (foam).

2. In a large bowl, stir the proofed yeast, oil, salt, and both flours to make a dough.

3. Place the dough onto a floured surface and knead 10 minutes.

4. Place the dough back into the bowl, cover, and let rise 2 hours.

5. Line the bottom of a 9x5-inch loaf pan with parchment paper.

6. Punch the dough down (yes, put your fist into it) and then place the dough onto a floured surface and knead a few minutes.

7. Place the dough into the prepared pan and let it rise 1 hour.

8. Preheat your oven to 350°F.

9. Place the bread into the oven and bake 50 minutes.

10. Remove the bread from the oven and let cool in the pan 10 minutes.

11. Remove the bread from the pan and let cool on a wire rack.

Apple Corn Muffins

(Makes 12)

One of the greatest things about homemade muffins is their total versatility. They can be a breakfast. They can be part of a healthy lunch or dinner, and even better, they are oftentimes a nutritional snack. Muffins are very cool, and luckily, they are easy and quick to make.

What I love about Southern types of muffins is how they will often incorporate seasonal fruits within the doughy little cups. A perfect example of this are these Apple Corn Muffins. Lush little gems of cornbread laced with the natural sweetness of apples. My grandmother used to serve these for breakfast right out of the oven, slathered with some butter and topped with maple syrup. Oh the good ol' days!

You can use any type of apple to make Apple Corn Muffins. I usually use a Golden Delicious or a Fuji. My grandmother would always use a Red Delicious. If you want a touch of tartness to the muffins, use a Granny Smith.

Ingredients

2 cups flour
½ cup yellow cornmeal
⅓ cup sugar
1 Tbs. baking powder
½ tsp. salt
1 cup milk
1 egg, beaten
¼ cup butter, melted
1 large apple (your choice of variety), peeled, cored, and diced

Steps

1. Preheat your oven to 425°F. Line a 12-cup muffin tin with paper cups.
2. In a medium bowl, whisk the flour, cornmeal, sugar, baking powder, and salt.
3. In another medium bowl, whisk the milk, egg, and butter.
4. Stir the milk mixture into the flour mixture.

5. Fold in the apple pieces.
6. Spoon into the prepared muffin tin, filling each cup about two-thirds full.
7. Place into the oven and bake 30 minutes.
8. Remove from the oven and let cool before eating.

Apple Muffins

(Makes 12 muffins)

Whereas our venture into Apple Corn Muffins (page 46) was a Southern type of muffin, these Apple Muffins are more of a Northwest type of muffin, and let's face a simple fact. The American Northwest knows their apples since some of the best tasting fruits come from this area of our great country.

Aside from the way in which these muffins are prepared, Apple Muffins also have a nice, slight hint of cinnamon to them. If you want a little deeper spice, you can also add a pinch of allspice to the festivities and that would make them a great autumn treat.

Since these Apple Muffins feature a little bit of spiciness to them, I would recommend making them with a sweeter red variety of apple. Personally, I think the famed Washington Red Delicious work just great, and if you can get them grown organically, there is no need to peel them before you dice them (but do remember to remove the core).

Ingredients
2 cups flour
½ cup sugar
2½ tsp. baking powder
1 tsp. ground cinnamon
½ tsp. salt
1¼ cups milk
¼ cup melted butter
1 egg, beaten
2 apples, peeled, cored, and diced

Steps
1. Preheat your oven to 400°F. Line a 12-cup muffin tin with paper cups.
2. Into a medium bowl, whisk the flour, sugar, baking powder, cinnamon, and salt.
3. In a separate medium bowl, whisk the milk, melted butter, and egg.
4. Stir the egg mixture into the flour mixture.

5. Fold in the apples.

6. Spoon the batter in the prepared muffin tin, filling each cup about two-thirds full.

7. Place into the oven and bake 20 minutes.

8. Remove from the oven and let cool before enjoying.

Applesauce Oat Muffins

(Makes 12 muffins)

One of the most classic American cakes is the famed applesauce cake. I do not know of anyone over the age of forty who did not have a mother or grandmother who would make this cake. These Applesauce Oat Muffins are very much like that beloved cake, and I think they will bring back a lot of memories.

Applesauce Oat Muffins became quite the popular fare in the Midwest for Sunday morning church gatherings. How the recipe actually came about is anyone's guess. Maybe someone was making simple applesauce muffins and some oats fell into the bowl . . . I don't know, but what I do know is these are really quite good, and they have a nice, slightly chewy texture (thanks to the oats). They also have more fiber than other muffins, and that is always a good thing.

I did make some adjustments to this recipe, and I will tell you why. The original recipe called for the addition of cream. I have changed it to half-and-half. The reason is: the heaviness of the cream weighed down the batter, and the muffins had a rather mushy texture. Not good! With the half-and-half, you still get the richness—without the added fat.

Ingredients

1 cup oats
1 cup applesauce
½ cup half-and-half
1 egg, beaten
1 tsp. vanilla
¼ cup melted butter
⅓ cup sugar
¾ cup flour
1 tsp. baking soda
1 tsp. ground cinnamon
¼ tsp. salt

Steps

1. Preheat your oven to 375°F. Line a 12-cup muffin tin with paper cups.
2. In a large bowl, vigorously stir the oats, applesauce, half-and-half, egg, vanilla, butter, and sugar.
3. In a small bowl, whisk the flour, baking soda, cinnamon, and salt.
4. Stir the flour mixture into the applesauce-oat mixture.
5. Spoon the batter into the prepared muffin tin, filling each cup about two-thirds full.
6. Place into the oven and bake 20 minutes.
7. Remove from the oven and let cool before enjoying.

Buttermilk Cornbread Muffins

(Makes 6 dinner muffins)

I don't think you can get more American than Buttermilk Cornbread Muffins, except for maybe the tried-and-true plain cornbread muffins—and those are coming up (page 57)! Buttermilk Cornbread Muffins have been a mainstay since the days of slavery in America, and though they may not be as popular now as they once were, you can bet your bottom dollar they are still served in some true Southern eateries.

This particular recipe for Buttermilk Cornbread Muffins is in no way like one of the originals. The originals were rather plain and somewhat hard. The reason for this is the fact they were served mostly with meals consisting of a gravy or sauce and the muffins were used to soak up the liquidly goodness. When they were served as a breakfast item, they were topped with a homemade Chicken Fried Steak Gravy (page 218) or Sausage Gravy (page 221).

These Buttermilk Cornbread Muffins are much lighter and have a wonderful aura of green onions and garlic to them. They are still wonderful served with chili or stew but they are also a joy to eat when slathered with some creamery fresh butter.

Ingredients

1 cup yellow cornmeal
⅓ cup flour
1 tsp. baking powder
1 tsp. salt
3 egg yolks
1 cup buttermilk
1 Tbs. lemon juice
2 scallions (green onions), minced
2 cloves garlic, minced

Steps

1. Preheat your oven to 400°F. Line a 6-cup jumbo muffin pan with paper cups.
2. In a medium bowl, whisk the cornmeal, flour, baking powder, and salt.
3. Stir in the egg yolks, buttermilk, lemon juice, scallions, and garlic.
4. Spoon the batter into the prepared muffin tin.
5. Place into the oven and bake 20 minutes.
6. Remove from the oven and let cool before enjoying.

English Muffins

(Makes 8 muffins)

I know what you're thinking. What are English Muffins doing in a book celebrating American food? It is a good question, and I have good answer. English Muffins are a version of an American griddle cake! Now, if I listed these as "Griddle Cakes," you might just pass this recipe by, so we'll call them by their most famous name, and that is English Muffins.

Most people have never had real English Muffins. They have had those awful things sold in plastic bags from the supermarket. Those are not English Muffins. Those are "stuff." English Muffins are a griddle cake, meaning they are prepared on a griddle or in a skillet. A true English Muffin has a texture you will not believe—they are airy, light, and almost melt in your mouth.

Now about those famed little "nooks and crannies" English Muffins are known for. Those come about due to the proper way of opening an English Muffin (a real one, not the "stuff" from supermarkets). Once the English Muffin is cooked, you poke the tines of a fork around the perimeter of the muffin. Then, with your fingertips, you pry it open. If you cut or slice through an English Muffin, you will not have the nooks and crannies.

Ingredients

1⅛ cups warm milk
1½ Tbs. butter
¾ tsp. salt
1 Tbs. sugar
1 egg, beaten
2¼ cups flour
1 tsp. yeast
yellow cornmeal to sprinkle on pan

Steps

1. In a mixer with the paddle attachment, add all the ingredients (except the cornmeal) and beat at medium speed for 5 minutes. The dough will be very sticky.

2. Place the dough into a bowl, cover, and let rise 2 hours.

3. Remove the dough from the bowl and place on a floured surface.

4. Divide the dough into 8 portions.

5. Pre-heat a griddle or skillet over low heat. Sprinkle the griddle or pan with some cornmeal (this will keep the muffins from sticking).

6. With floured hands, pat each portion of dough into a disc about 4-inches thick.

7. Place the English Muffins on the griddle or pan and cook about 10 minutes per side.

8. Remove the English Muffins to a wire rack and let cool slightly before opening them up (see note above).

Nut Bran Muffins

(Makes 12 muffins)

These muffins may be one of the most classic of American sweet muffins. I remember my mother making these muffins whenever she bought a box of All-Bran® cereal. This was before they started to add boatloads of chemicals to cereals, but the good news is that you can still buy organic bran cereal—and if you do, by all means, make these tasty little muffins.

For my money, these are one of the better breakfast muffins ever created because not only are they a wonderful way to start the day, they are also quite nutritious. You have a lot of fiber in these muffins, and you actually have a decent amount of vitamins and minerals with the raisins and the walnuts. Since they contain brown sugar and not the usual white sugar, they are not as sweet, but they do have a nice richness to them.

This recipe is for the little muffins. The type some of us grew up with. The same size as a normal cupcake. This is the perfect size for breakfast. Two of these to start your day with a cup of coffee—and you are ready for anything!

Ingredients

½ cup bran cereal

⅔ cup milk

½ cup brown sugar, divided

2 Tbs. dark corn syrup, divided

5 Tbs. melted butter, divided

⅓ cup chopped walnuts

⅓ cup raisins

2 Tbs. molasses

1 egg, beaten

1½ cups flour

Steps

1. Preheat your oven to 400°F. Line a 12-cup muffin tin with paper cups.

2. In a small bowl, combine the bran cereal and milk. Set the bowl aside 5 minutes for the cereal to soften.

3. In a small saucepan over medium heat, stir ¼ cup brown sugar, 2 teaspoons corn syrup, and 2 tablespoons melted butter until the brown sugar has dissolved.

4. Spoon some of this syrup into each of the paper cups in the muffin tin.

5. In a large bowl, combine all remaining ingredients and stir until batter forms.

6. Fill each muffin cup two-thirds full with the batter.

7. Place into the oven and bake 15 minutes.

8. Remove from the oven and let cool before enjoying.

All-American Corn Muffins

(Makes 6 dinner muffins)

When it comes to corn muffins, these are the one which most people will remember. A nothing-fancy corn muffin relying solely on the taste of the cornmeal. This is the corn muffin of history. These are truly Americana.

When you are in the kitchen making these muffins, you will be doing exactly what your grand- or great grandmother would have been doing on any evening. She'd be standing over the stove, making cornmeal and then adding some simple ingredients to turn them into corn muffins. They might not have been eating them at the Ritz in New York City, but they sure were enjoying them in small-town rural America.

When I make these All-American Corn Muffins, I like to enjoy them really simply and probably the way most people ate them way back when. While they are still warm, slice them and slather some sweet butter on them. Then drizzle them with some honey and get ready to taste some American food history.

Ingredients
2 cups yellow cornmeal
1 tsp. salt
2 cups boiling water
1 Tbs. butter
1 egg, beaten
1 cup milk
1 tsp. baking powder

Steps
1. Preheat your oven to 400°F. Line a 6-cup jumbo muffin pan with paper cups.
2. In a large bowl, whisk the cornmeal, salt, and boiling water until there are no lumps.
3. Stir in the butter and then set the bowl aside to cool.
4. Into the cooled mixture, stir the egg, milk, and baking powder. Let the mixture rest 10 minutes.
5. Spoon the batter into the prepared muffin tin, filling each cup about two-thirds full.
6. Place the muffins into the oven and bake 30 minutes.
7. Remove the muffins from the oven and let cool before enjoying.

By the Bowl

Chilis, Soups, and Stews

Beef and Brew Stew

(Serves 4)

By all accounts, this stew is a Texas original, and I think it might be a pretty good bet to say its origins probably came about because some drunk cowboy was making stew and dropped his longneck bottle of beer into the pot. I don't know for a fact; I am just guessing. Regardless, it is damn good!

From looking at the ingredients here, you might think this is along the lines of a chili. You might be right, but remember, this is from Texas, and they already have too many chilis! So if something is slightly different, it gets called a "stew." This is Texas Cooking 101.

You can actually use any type of beer you want to make this stew. This recipe calls for a dark variety of beer, and that is for two reasons: first, the color will enrich the look of the stew; secondly, dark beers are usually more flavorful and robust, thus pairing better with the beef.

By the way, if you don't know what a parsnip is, it is the white carrot-looking thing in the produce section of your market. They taste like a cross between a carrot and parsley and are quite delicious!

Ingredients

6 pieces bacon, chopped
2 Tbs. cornstarch
2 tsp. chili powder
1 tsp. celery salt
1 tsp. dry mustard
1 tsp. ground cumin
½ tsp. ground cayenne pepper
2½ pounds stew meat, cubed
2 yellow onions, chopped
2 cups dark beer
2 cups beef stock
2 Tbs. tomato paste
6 parsnips, peeled and chopped
6 carrots, peeled and chopped
2 potatoes, peeled and cubed

Steps

1. Preheat your oven to 325°F.

2. In a large sauté pan or skillet, cook the bacon over medium heat. Remove the bacon and set aside. Leave the bacon fat in the pan and keep the pan on the heat.

3. In a large ziplock bag, add the cornstarch, chili powder, celery salt, dry mustard, cumin, and cayenne pepper and shake to blend.

4. Add the beef to the spice mixture and shake the bag to dredge (coat) the meat.

5. Place the meat into the rendered bacon fat and brown it on all sides.

6. Remove the beef and place into a 4-quart oven-proof pot.

7. Into the pot, add the onions, beer, beef stock, and tomato paste. Stir the ingredients to blend them.

8. Place the pot into the oven and cook 90 minutes.

9. Add the remaining ingredients to the pot, place back into the oven, and cook 90 minutes longer.

10. Remove from the oven, spoon into bowls, and enjoy.

Beer Chili

(Serves 4)

Beer Chili has been a staple in many American diners for quite some time, and the reason is really quite simple. It has the word "beer" in the title. There is just something about marketing "beer" into a title which makes it popular . . . like beer nuts!

Where Beer Chili originated is a subject which can cause quite a few arguments. We do know it originated somewhere in the great American Southwest, and this makes sense since this area used to have a great selection of diners and truck-stops. One of the great dinners for many truckers would be a big bowl of Beer Chili and an endless supply of corn muffins (and coffee).

Beer Chili contains beans, which would lead some people to say it shouldn't be called a chili. There have actually been fistfights over the inclusion of beans in chili. I say, just chill out! Beans or no beans, a good bowl of chili warms anyone's heart. The beans for this chili are pinto beans, and I think the pinto bean is perfect here, so don't go substituting the kidney bean.

Ingredients

1 pound ground beef
1 yellow onion, chopped
4 cloves garlic, minced
1 15-ounce can pinto beans, drained
2 8-ounce cans tomato sauce
12-ounce bottle beer (any variety)
¼ cup tomato paste
¾ cup beef stock

1 Tbs. chili powder
1 tsp. ground cumin
1 tsp. hot sauce

Steps

1. In a large pot over medium-high heat, cook the ground beef, onion, and garlic 10 minutes.

2. Lower the heat to medium and stir in the pinto beans and remaining ingredients.

3. Bring the chili to a boil.

4. Reduce the heat to a simmer and cook the chili 90 minutes (add water or stock if it gets too thick).

Tomato Soup

(Serves 6)

I don't really know how to break this news, so forgive my bluntness. Tomato soup does not come in cans. Seriously, have you ever seen a tomato look anything like what plops out of those cans? No, you haven't. Actually, what does come out of those cans is a Tomato Gravy, and I will prove this fact in the chapter entitled America's Gravies (page 222), where I will show you how to make it. This Tomato Soup features tomatoes (gasp!), and you will actually taste them.

Tomato Soup is not an American dish, but we Americans sure do love it. There are many variations of Tomato Soup with each section of America claiming their own. This version, fresh and vibrant, is quite popular throughout the Northwest, and I am sure it originated in a farmhouse kitchen just by the way it is presented.

You can use any variety of tomato to make this soup. I really like using Roma tomatoes as they are fleshier, and I think have a more vibrant flavor. If using Romas, I would increase the amount of tomatoes to eight. I have never made this soup with any of the heirloom tomatoes on the market, but I am sure they would work quite well.

Ingredients

2 Tbs. butter
1 leek, cleaned and chopped
4 large tomatoes, chopped
2 cups chicken stock

2 cups beef stock
⅓ cup minced fresh basil

Steps

1. Melt the butter in a medium saucepan over medium heat.

2. Add the leek and sauté 5 minutes.

3. Stir in the tomatoes and cook 5 minutes.

4. Stir in the chicken and beef stock and bring to a boil.

5. Reduce the heat to a simmer and cook 30 minutes.

6. Remove the soup from the heat.

7. Ladle into bowls, sprinkle with basil, and enjoy.

Chicken Chili

(Serves 4)

How did Chicken Chili come about? I'm glad you asked because I have the answer. It was created in the diners of America as a way to use leftover chicken (fried or roasted). There was a time in America when food waste was almost considered sinful, and the diners and truck stops from sea to shining sea would create dishes using whatever was left over from the previous day's menu. Many of these dishes have become American classics . . . like Chicken Chili!

As mentioned above, this is the perfect dish to use leftover chicken. Simply remove the skin from the chicken (never good the next day) and either chop or shred the meat. You can also make this recipe with leftover turkey or any other fowl.

If you're looking for a spicy hot chili, Chicken Chili is not the chili for you. This is very tame, though still quite tasty with only a subtle flavoring of chili. If you want it to be hotter, use four serrano peppers instead of the green bell pepper. This is a wonderful chili to serve over some grilled polenta or any of the cornbreads featured in this book.

Ingredients

2 Tbs. corn oil
1 yellow onion, chopped
1 green bell pepper, chopped
2 stalks celery, chopped
4 cloves garlic, minced
2 Tbs. chili powder
2 tsp. ground cumin
2 cups chicken stock
2 15-ounce cans pinto beans, drained
2 cups chopped or shredded leftover chicken
½ cup half-and-half

Steps

1. Heat the oil in a large saucepan over medium heat.
2. Add the onion, bell pepper, and celery and sauté 5 minutes.
3. Stir in the garlic, chili powder, and cumin and cook 1 minute.
4. Stir in the stock and bring to a boil.

5. Reduce the heat to a simmer and cook 5 minutes.

6. Stir in the pinto beans, chicken, and half-and-half and cook 15 minutes.

7. Ladle into bowls and enjoy!

Chili Gravy

(Serves 4)

Honestly, I have no idea why this chili is called a gravy. What I do know is it is incredibly tasty, simple to make, and when served over mashed potatoes (an old diner dish) or rice, it makes for a great dinner. This is another chili which hails from the great state of Texas and has been adapted throughout the years with some very tasty touches of the great American Southwest.

When you make this chili, you are going to be learning how to make a real chili sauce by reconstituting some dried chilies. This is always good to know; it is very simple to do and, in the long run, will end up saving you quite a bit of money if you like or use chili sauces often.

Chili Gravy is one of the few "real" chili dishes which calls for ground beef (hamburger). Since most ground beef sold in markets doesn't have enough fat in it to make it tasty (yes, fat equals taste), I would recommend grinding your own beef. It is a little more work but the results are so much more flavorful and you will actually end up saving quite a bit of money.

Ingredients

6 dried ancho chilies
6 dried New Mexico chilies
4 cups beef stock
1 pound ground beef
1 yellow onion, minced
4 cloves garlic, minced
1 Tbs. ground cumin
2 tsp. dried oregano
½ tsp. salt
1 Tbs. yellow cornmeal

Steps

1. Remove the stem ends of the dried chilies. Using kitchen scissors, cut the chilies down the middle and remove the seeds and discard them.

2. In a medium saucepan, bring the beef stock to a boil over medium heat.

3. Add the dried chilies to the stock. Remove the stock from the heat and let sit until the dried chilies have softened (reconstituted).

4. Place the dried chilies and the stock into a food processor or blender and puree. Do this in batches. Alternatively, you may use an immersion blender directly in the pot (if you use an immersion blender, remove the pureed peppers to a bowl before proceeding to the next step).

5. In the same medium saucepan over medium heat, add the ground beef, onion, and garlic and cook 10 minutes. Drain off any rendered fat.

6. Stir in the cumin, oregano, salt, and pureed peppers and any remaining stock and bring to a boil.

7. Reduce the heat to a simmer and cook 50 minutes.

8. Stir in the cornmeal and cook 10 minutes. The cornmeal will slightly thicken the Chili Gravy.

9. Spoon into serving bowls and enjoy.

Corn Chowder

(Serves 4)

Like any great chowder, this Corn Chowder originated in the Northeast portion of America, and unless you want to be made fun of, you would always order it not as "chowder" but as "chowda." I'm serious!

There is nothing better than a good hearty Corn Chowder. For it to have the ultimate in taste and texture, the corn must be of the sweet variety, and it must be freshly shucked (meaning the corn must be fresh and the kernels removed from the cob just before making). It is very important to remember one simple trick for perfect Corn Chowder. Once the kernels are removed, take the back of the knife (the noncutting edge), and scrape it along the cob to remove the naturally sweet corn milk. This gets added to the "chowda" along with the corn.

What is the difference between a "chowder" and a "soup"? You will get differing answers to this question depending on who you ask. For reasons of simplicity, the reason is the thickness. Another bone of contention regarding chowders is the type of potato to use. I will use any potato I have in the kitchen, which usually means a typical Russet.

Ingredients

6 slices of bacon, chopped
2 sweet yellow onions, chopped
2 Tbs. flour
4 cups chicken stock
2 potatoes, peeled and diced
1 cup cream
4 cups freshly shucked sweet corn kernels

Steps

1. In a medium saucepan over medium heat, cook the bacon until crisp. Remove the bacon from the pan and set aside.

2. Into the saucepan with the rendered bacon fat, add the onions and sauté 10 minutes.

3. Stir in the flour and cook 2 minutes.

4. Add the chicken stock and potatoes and simmer 30 minutes or until the potatoes are fork tender.

5. Stir in the cream and corn and simmer 10 minutes.

6. Ladle into serving bowls and enjoy.

Firestarter Chili

(Serves 4)

Don't you just love the name of this chili? Firestarter Chili—just the name beckons those old Hollywood comedies where the people would eat the hot chili and then smoke would come out of their ears. Well, names can be deceiving because this chili is not really that hot, but it is awfully damned good.

This chili is an American diner–conceived chili and thus the name. During the heyday of American diners, they always had some great names for their dishes. Names which were exciting and made you want to order the dish, like Firestarter Chili, which many times was served with Atomic Fries (which were nothing more than thick-cut french fries).

When this dish was made in the diners, they always used the cheapest cut of beef they could find, which makes sense since you won't really be tasting the beef. Also, it will be cooked for a long period of time, so the beef doesn't have to come from a tender part of the cow. The best cut of beef to use for chili is chuck roll, which is available at all markets for a decent price.

Ingredients

¼ cup corn oil

3 pounds chuck roll, trimmed of excess fat and cubed

1 red onion, chopped

4 cloves garlic, minced

¼ cup chili powder

1 Tbs. ground cumin

2 tsp. salt

2 tsp. hot sauce

3 cups water

8 jalapeño peppers, minced (remove seeds for less heat)

Steps

1. Heat the oil in a large saucepan over medium heat.
2. Add the beef and brown on all sides (do this in batches if necessary).
3. Remove the browned beef and set aside. Into the saucepan, add the onion and garlic and sauté 5 minutes.
4. Stir in the chili powder, cumin, salt, and hot sauce and cook 2 minutes.
5. Stir in the water and peppers and bring to a boil.
6. Add the beef and bring the chili to a simmer.
7. Reduce the heat to low and cook 90 minutes.
8. Ladle into bowls and enjoy.

Cream of Mushroom Soup

(Serves 4)

I think one of the saddest things in life is that the majority of Americans only know Cream of Mushroom Soup from cans. Coagulated gunk is not soup. There was a time in America's history when diners and many restaurants made their own soups from scratch, using the leftovers from the previous day. Those days are now gone, but you can make your own soups at home in very little time and for very little money.

I am a huge fan of Cream of Mushroom Soup. It is a soup which is very hearty, very rich, and because it is creamed the natural way—with cream—it is also pretty high up there on the calorie counter, but that is why you are only supposed to serve a small cup of it.

To make a perfect and authentic Cream of Mushroom soup, you must first learn to make a basic food item called a "roux." A roux is a natural thickener for soups (or gravies). Yes, it is a French culinary word, but don't let that intimidate you because a roux is simply a combination of butter and flour. In the steps to this dish, I'll walk you through making a roux, and thus you can become the next Julia Child!

Ingredients

3 Tbs. butter
6 scallions (green onions), minced
1 Tbs. flour
3 cups chicken stock
1 pound small mushrooms, chopped
¾ cup cream
salt and pepper, to taste

Steps

1. In a medium saucepan over medium heat, melt the butter.
2. Add the scallions and sauté 3 minutes.
3. Stir in the flour and cook 1 minute. (You just made a roux!)
4. Remove the saucepan from the heat and whisk in the chicken stock until the texture is smooth and silky.
5. Place the saucepan back onto the heat and stir in the mushrooms until the soup comes to a boil.
6. Reduce the heat to a simmer and cook 10 minutes.

7. Stir in the cream, season to taste with salt and pepper, and bring just to the simmer point.

8. Ladle into bowls and enjoy.

Green Chili Stew

(Serves 4)

I always love when I order a "green" chili, and when it is served to me, it isn't green. In my mind, I am always screaming, "Then why call it green?!" Well, the answer is simple (yet still aggravating), and it is because green chilies are used. Regardless, green chili is a good chili and usually not as hot as a typical bowl of red.

As you will notice, this is a chili stew. What does this mean? Hell if I know! This particular Green Chili Stew hails from the South, and it might be for this reason that the word "stew" is in the title. In the South, they love their stews, and they make some of the best you will ever eat. They are not, however, the best chili makers in the known world. When you take these two points under consideration, this may be why it is called a "chili stew."

For this recipe, we are going to use canned whole tomatoes. You will want an organic variety, not only for taste but also because the juice will not contain extra sugar or salt. When you use these tomatoes, break them up with your hands. Sort of squash them in your palms with the pulp running between your fingers. Not only is this fun, it will also give you the perfect texture for the Green Chili Stew.

Ingredients

1 Tbs. corn oil
2½ pounds pork butt, trimmed of excess fat and cubed
2 yellow onions, chopped
6 cloves garlic, minced
¼ cup chili powder
1 Tbs. ground cumin
1 tsp. ground coriander
2 28-ounce cans whole tomatoes, with their juice
1 tsp. salt
6 jalapeño peppers, minced (seeds removed for less heat)
2 cups water
1 Tbs. yellow cornmeal

Steps

1. In a large saucepan, heat the oil over medium heat.
2. Add the pork and brown on all sides.

3. Add the onions, garlic, chili powder, cumin, and coriander and cook 5 minutes.

4. Break up the tomatoes with your hands and add them along with their juices and cook 2 minutes.

5. Stir in the salt and jalapeño peppers and cook 5 minutes.

6. In a small bowl, whisk the water and the cornmeal.

7. Stir the cornmeal mixture into the chili and bring to a boil while stirring.

8. Lower the heat to a simmer and cook 1 hour.

9. Ladle into bowls and enjoy.

Ham and Bean Soup

(Serves 4)

Ham and Bean Soup is one of the most popular American soups to ever be devised. No matter whether you went to a diner, a truck stop, a greasy spoon, or your favorite local eatery, the chances are very strong that once or twice a week their soup of the day would be Ham and Bean. Why? It costs almost nothing to make (the ham was usually leftover), and people loved it—easy profit!

In making this Ham and Bean Soup, we are going to go old school. No using canned white beans. We are going to use dried beans, and I will take you through the course of preparing them. It is very simple, but it does take twenty-four hours. It is important to know how to make beans the old-fashioned way, and it can save you quite a bit of money since the canned beans are sometimes just downright expensive.

About the ham for this soup—you have many choices. You can use leftover ham from a holiday dinner (which would be a picnic ham variety). You can use a deli style ham, or you can use my favorite, smoked ham hocks. If using a smoked ham hocks, just remember to remove the meat from the bone before serving the soup.

Ingredients

2 cups dried white beans
6 cloves garlic, minced
1 cup chopped celery
2 yellow onions, chopped
½ cup tomato sauce
2 cups chopped or shredded smoked ham (or 6 smoked ham hocks)

Steps

1. Place the dried beans in a large bowl and cover them with cold water. Let the beans soak overnight.

2. After 24 hours of soaking, drain the beans and discard the soaking water.

3. In a large pot over high heat, add the beans, garlic, celery, onions, tomato sauce, and ham with just enough water to cover them by 1½ inches. Bring the soup to a boil.

4. Reduce the heat to a simmer and cook 2 hours (during the cooking process, skim off any foam which may appear).

5. If needed, add more water during the last portion of cooking.

6. Ladle into bowls and enjoy.

Ranch Stew

(Serves 4)

Who doesn't love a piping hot bowl of beef stew? There is just something about chowing down on chunks of beef and veggies in a thick and rich liquid that warms the cockles of even the coldest heart. Stews are an American tradition, and for the best of them, we can thank the cowboys (no, not the Dallas ones).

This version of beef stew we call Ranch Stew is a very popular dish at dude ranches throughout America, albeit each dude ranch will have its own adaptation. This has everything you love about a stew in it. There is the beef, the veggies, and the potatoes. There is also a secret little ingredient which really makes this stew stand out, and that is a hefty addition of strong coffee.

When it comes to stews, you have your choice of breads to serve with them. It can either be cornbread or biscuits—you only want these for two simple reasons: first, it is the American way to eat stew, and secondly, both of them can sop up the yummy gravy to absolute perfection.

Ingredients

1½ pounds stew meat, cubed
6 Tbs. flour
2 Tbs. corn oil
1½ cups coffee (the stronger the better)
2 Tbs. brown sugar
4 cloves garlic, minced
1 Tbs. dried oregano, crumbled
1 tsp. chili powder
4 carrots, chopped
2 onions, chopped
2 potatoes, diced
4 ribs celery, chopped
1¾ cups water

Steps

1. Place the beef and flour into a large bowl and toss the beef until it is dredged (coated).
2. Heat the oil in a large sauté pan over medium heat. Add the beef and brown on all sides.

3. Stir in the coffee, brown sugar, garlic, oregano, and chili powder and bring to a boil.

4. Reduce the heat to a simmer, cover the pan, and cook 90 minutes.

5. Add the carrots, onions, potatoes, celery, and water.

6. Bring the stew to a simmer and cook 35 minutes.

7. Ladle into bowls and enjoy.

Red Bean Soup

(Serves 4)

There was a time in America when beans were the food of choice for most people. This was usually during times of great economic woes, as beans were always a cheap food (and in many cases, they still are today). Beans are also one of the wonder foods from nature as they are truly a potent little nutrition bomb, featuring high amount of vitamins, mineral, fiber, and very little fat. Beans rock!

Red Bean Soup was a very popular soup throughout the Midwest and the South. What is a red bean? It is a kidney bean! When this soup was made at various diners and eateries, they always did it the old-fashioned way, meaning they soaked the beans overnight and then precooked the beans before making the soup. Since kidney beans are so inexpensive by the can these days, make it simple for yourself and use the canned variety, but remember to drain them and rinse them under cold running water.

You can use either smoked ham which has been chopped or ham hocks to make this soup. I prefer to use smoked ham hocks as I think they add more flavor, but they also add more work. If using ham hocks, remove them before you puree the soup and then remove the meat from the bones, adding the meat back to the soup after it has been pureed.

Ingredients

4 ham hocks (or 2 cups smoked ham, chopped)
2 yellow onions, chopped
4 scallions (green onions), chopped
3 ribs celery, chopped
3 Tbs. chopped parsley
5 cloves garlic, chopped
½ green bell pepper, chopped
4 quarts water
1 Tbs. salt
2 tsp. ground black pepper
¼ tsp. cayenne pepper
1 Tbs. chopped thyme
3 whole bay leaves
2 cans kidney beans, drained and rinsed

Steps

1. In a large saucepan over high heat, combine all of the ingredients, except the kidney beans, and bring to a boil.

2. Reduce the heat to a simmer and cook 2 hours.

3. Place the kidney beans into the soup and cook 15 minutes.

4. Remove the pan from the heat. Remove the bay leaves and discard. Remove the ham hocks (or smoked ham) from the soup and set aside to cool.

5. Puree the soup in either a food processor or blender (in batches) and place back into the pan. Alternatively, you may use an immersion blender directly in the pot.

6. If you're using ham hocks, remove the meat and discard the bones. Place the meat back into the soup and bring the soup to a simmer over medium heat.

7. Remove the soup from the heat, ladle into bowls, and enjoy.

Sausage and Beef Stew

(Serves 4)

There is an expression in the great American Midwest that refers to food as "rib-sticking." This simply suggests food which is hearty and stays with you (doesn't burn off fast). These types of food are very important in areas of America which have pretty harsh winters and is one of the reasons why this part of America has some of the best stews you will ever enjoy—such as this Sausage and Beef Stew.

You can use any type of sausage you like to make this dish. I prefer to use kielbasa as I think it not only handles the cooking process perfectly, but the spices which make this sausage so tasty also blend well with the other ingredients. The texture of kielbasa is also a nice counter to the texture of the beef.

This stew does contain wine. If you are your guests have any type of alcohol-related illness, you can skip the wine and instead use 2 extra cups of beef stock mixed with a cup of water. The flavor and richness will be a little off, but it will still be quite delicious. Do NOT use that stuff called non-alcohol wine; it is disgusting!

Ingredients

1 pound kielbasa sausage, sliced
2½ pounds beef stew meat, cubed
1 Tbs. flour
3 Tbs. butter
1 Tbs. olive oil
4 yellow onions, thinly sliced
4 cloves garlic, minced
3 cups red wine (your choice), or 2 cups beef stock mixed with 1 cup water
2 cups beef stock
3 sprigs parsley
2 bay leaves
2 tsp. dried thyme, crumbled
5 carrots, sliced
5 parsnips, sliced
1½ cups water
2 tsp. sugar
½ tsp. salt

Steps

1. In a large saucepan over medium-high heat, add the sausage and beef and brown on all sides. Remove the sausage and beef and set aside.

2. Into the pan, add the flour, butter, olive oil, onions, and garlic and sauté 5 minutes.

3. Place the sausage, beef, wine, stock, parsley, bay leaves, and thyme into the pan, cover, and cook 30 minutes.

4. Add the carrots, parsnips, water, sugar, and salt and cook 40 minutes.

5. Remove the bay leaves and parsley sprigs and discard.

6. Remove the stew from the heat, ladle into bowls, and enjoy.

Smoked Sausage and Lentil Soup

(Serves 4)

No one really knows how lentils came to America other than the fact that they were obviously from Europeans. Also, no one knows where the first lentil soup was made in America, but the chances are rather great it was somewhere on the East Coast. Regardless of what no one knows, lentil soup has always been popular, and when you add some smoked sausage to the pot, it becomes downright American!

Lentils are a legume, which means they are part of the bean family. Lentils are also one of the most powerful foods you can put into your body. They are considered one of nature's wonder foods. Another point, and this is rather important, is the fact that lentils are cheap! Lentils come in various colors (they all taste the same), but the ones I like to use for this soup are the common brownish ones. Remember to pick through the lentils before cooking with them because there are often little stones in the package.

You can use any type of smoked sausage for this soup. I prefer the spicier versions. I have also had this with thick chunks of bacon. It was very good, but I guess you couldn't call it Smoked Sausage and Lentil Soup anymore. Serve this with some cornbread for a wonderful autumn or winter dinner.

Ingredients

8 cups water
2 cups lentils, rinsed and picked clean
1 tsp. corn oil
2 pounds smoked sausage, chopped
2 yellow onions, chopped
8 cloves garlic, minced
4 cups chicken stock
1 bunch spinach, chopped
4 tomatoes, diced

Steps

1. In a large pot over high heat, bring the 8 cups of water to a boil. Add the lentils, lower the heat to a simmer, cover, and cook 1 hour. The lentils will soak up most of the water.

2. In a medium sauté pan, heat the oil over medium heat. Add the sausage and cook until done. Remove the sausage and set aside.

3. Into the pan, add the onions and sauté 5 minutes. Add the garlic and sauté 2 minutes. Remove the pan from the heat.

4. Add the chicken stock, sausage, and onion mixture to the lentils and then stir in the spinach and tomatoes.

5. Bring the soup to a simmer and cook 15 minutes.

6. Ladle into bowls and enjoy.

··· **Note** ···

Once the lentils have cooked, you will notice they have taken in most, if not all, of the water they were cooked in. This is why you will add the chicken stock.

Split Pea and Smoked Bacon Soup

(Serves 4)

There are many people who believe that split pea soup is an American original. It is not. It is actually French by origin; however, it is one of the most popular soups from the heyday of American diners and local eateries. It is also, in my opinion, one of the finer soups for the soul as, for many, it is also a grand comfort food.

This particular Split Pea and Smoked Bacon Soup is sort of a compilation of all the ones I have found which were made in some of the most well-known diners and roadside eateries. If you are a split pea aficionado, you will notice something interesting about this recipe. It contains potatoes. I have asked a couple of food historians about this, and no one really knows why they're included. I will assume it was to use potatoes before they went bad.

Another interesting aspect of this soup is the fact that it is not pureed. Yes, this is a split pea soup that has a real texture. I have had it a few times exactly as I am presenting it here, and it is very good. It gets its thickness and creamy texture from the length of cooking time, which will naturally "cream" the split peas. It is quite thick. If you want it more "soupy," just add more stock (or water) during the last 5 minutes of cooking.

Ingredients

1½ cups dried green split peas

6 cups chicken stock

2 cloves garlic, minced

1 Tbs. minced oregano

¼ tsp. ground white pepper

1 bay leaf

½ pound smoked bacon, cooked and chopped

2 carrots, chopped

1 yellow onion, chopped

2 potatoes, peeled and cubed

2 ribs celery, chopped

Steps

1. In a large saucepan over medium heat, combine the split peas, chicken stock, garlic, oregano, white pepper, and bay leaf.

2. Lower the heat to a simmer, cover, and cook 1 hour.

3. Stir in the bacon, carrots, onion, potatoes, and celery and bring to a boil.

4. Reduce the heat to a simmer, cover, and cook 30 minutes.

5. Remove the soup from the heat and discard the bay leaf.

6. Ladle into bowls and enjoy.

Sweet Potato Soup

(Serves 4)

I remember when I was growing up that I hated potato soup. Then, somewhere along the line, I grew up, matured (okay, that is still to be debated), and started loving potato soup. I think this may have occurred somewhere between Utah and Kansas; during a family trip to see relatives in Arkansas, we stopped at every diner along the way (or so it seemed), and they all had potato soup as their soup of the day.

This potato soup is made with sweet potatoes, which might make you think its origins are in the South. True there are many soups featuring sweet potatoes from the South, but this one is strictly California. The first time I had a Sweet Potato Soup was at this little café in St. Helena, California. I loved the freshness and the texture (slightly creamier than a normal potato soup). I really didn't want the bowl to ever empty!

For this version of Sweet Potato Soup, I decided to play with flavors. I also wanted a slightly more vibrant color. I achieved both by adding one very simple ingredient: orange juice. Though sweet potatoes are thought of as an autumn food, I think this soup makes for a wonderful brunch dish on a Spring day when served with some sourdough French bread and a perfectly chilled white wine (so California, I know).

Ingredients

3 large sweet potatoes, peeled and cubed
3 cups chicken stock
½ cup orange juice
2 Tbs. dark spicy mustard
1 tsp. salt
½ tsp. ground black pepper
¼ tsp. cayenne
2 Tbs. sour cream (or plain yogurt)

Steps

1. In a medium saucepan, combine the sweet potatoes and stock and bring to a boil.
2. Reduce the heat to a simmer and cook 20 minutes or until the sweet potatoes are fork-tender.
3. Place the stock and potatoes into a food processor or blender and puree (in batches).

4. Return the puree back to the pan and bring to a simmer.
5. Stir in the orange juice, mustard, salt, pepper, cayenne, and sour cream.
6. Bring the soup just to the point of a simmer and then remove it from the heat.
7. Ladle into bowls and enjoy.

Texas Chili

(Serves 4)

A word about the chilies of Texas. There is an official Texas chili for every resident of the Lone Star State, or so it seems. You can go into every diner, roadhouse, café, truck stop, or eatery of your choice in this state, and you will find on the menu a Texas Chili. They do indeed love their chili in Texas, but they just cannot come to an agreement on an official one.

Chili: Should it have beans or not? Believe it or not, there have actually been murders over this question. My answer is simple. Yes and no! Yes, if you like beans in your chili, and no, if you don't. This Texas Chili has beans. If you don't like beans, make it without the beans.

One thing all chili fans, even in Texas, will agree to is the fact that a chili should be thick and robust. You should be able to eat a chili with a fork and leave the bowl clean. Should a chili be spicy hot? Actually, no, it shouldn't be (although I have had great chilies that made my tongue scream). What it should be is perfectly balanced with spices. So . . . here is my version of Texas Chili!

Ingredients

1½ Tbs. corn oil
2 pounds beef chuck roll, trimmed of excess fat and cubed
¼ cup chili powder
4 cloves garlic, minced
1 tsp. ground coriander
1 Tbs. ground cumin
1 tsp. salt
1 cup water
2 cups beef stock
4 cups canned pinto beans, drained and rinsed
1 white onion, minced

Steps:

1. In a large saucepan, heat the oil over medium heat.
2. Add the beef and brown on all sides.
3. In a medium bowl, whisk the chili powder, garlic, coriander, cumin, salt, and water.

4. Stir the chili powder mixture into the pan and cook 5 minutes.
5. Stir in the beef stock and bring to a boil.
6. Reduce the heat to a simmer and cook 1 hour.
7. Add the pinto beans and onion and bring the chili to a boil.
8. Reduce the heat to a simmer and cook 20 minutes.
9. Remove the chili from the heat.
10. Ladle into bowls and enjoy.

Baked Corn

(Serves 4)

Corn is one of the most popular produce items in America. During the course of corn season, the produce sections of supermarkets throughout the United States are lined with bales of corn—white and yellow and sweet and regular. Americans love their corn, and it is a good thing because it is also one of the most versatile foods as will be proven by the time you get to the end of this masterpiece of American cookery.

Though there are Baked Corn dishes which actually call for you to bake ears of corn, this is not one of them. This is more along the lines of a casserole, and casseroles make for some of the best side dishes around. For those of you into those recipes known as "one-pot-meals," you will fall in love with casseroles because they indeed are the original American "one-pot-meal."

I recommend using fresh corn whenever possible. The flavor cannot be beat, and the texture will always have a nice and fresh crunch to it. If it is not corn season, a good alternative is frozen corn as long as it has been flash-frozen. When it comes to the canned variety of corns, I have never tasted one which even came close to being fresh. As far as the fresh corn for this dish, I always use a sweet variety of white corn.

Ingredients

1 Tbs. corn oil
1 sweet yellow onion, chopped
1 rib celery, chopped
2 Tbs. butter
2 Tbs. chili powder
2 cups tomato sauce
3 cups fresh sweet white corn
1 tsp. salt
½ tsp. ground black pepper
¼ cup grated Monterey Jack cheese

Steps

1. Preheat your oven to 350°F.

2. In a medium sauté pan, heat the oil over medium heat. Add the onion and celery and sauté 5 minutes.

3. Stir in the butter, chili powder, tomato sauce, corn, salt, and pepper and cook 5 minutes.

4. Spoon the mixture into an oven-proof casserole dish.

5. Top the mixture with the cheese and cover with foil.

6. Place into the oven and bake 45 minutes.

7. Remove the foil and bake 15 minutes.

8. Remove from the oven and let cool slightly before serving.

Smoked Ham and Potato Leek Soup

(Serves 4)

A long, long time ago and in a galaxy far, far away, I worked at the famed Palace Hotel in San Francisco. The chef in charge of soups there was a man from Germany named Frank, and he was brilliant in his craft. He would make this soup about twice a month, and it would sell out every time. He never did give me his recipe, but through the years of attempting to recreate it, I have come up with something close and this is it.

When you make this soup, it is very important to use a good quality smoked ham. If you use one of the cheap types of ham, you will not get a full-bodied flavor, and the slight smokiness will taste fake. This is not a good thing. You can either cube the ham (which makes it easier to get into the spoon), or you can do what I often do and slice it julienne-style (very thin matchstick slices), which makes it harder to get into a spoon but makes for a better soup.

The only potato I recommend for this soup is a very simple Russet potato. They cook perfectly without losing their stability, and they also "cream" better once you mash half of them (for texture).

Ingredients

3 Tbs. butter
4 leeks, washed and chopped
3 cups chicken stock

2 large potatoes, peeled and cubed
½ pound good quality smoked ham, cubed

Steps

1. In a large sauce pan, melt the butter over medium heat.

2. Add the leeks and sauté 10 minutes.

3. Stir in the stock and potatoes and bring to a boil.

4. Reduce the heat to a simmer and cook 15 minutes or until the potatoes are tender enough to mash.

5. Using a potato masher, mash half of the potatoes and then stir them to incorporate them into the soup.

6. Add the smoked ham and simmer 5 minutes.

7. Ladle into bowls and enjoy.

On the Side

Accompaniments

Black-Eyed Peas

(Serves 6)

Grab a hat and some boots and sharpen your drawl, we're heading to the deep South and one of the most popular side dishes to ever come from this part of America, and we're going to do it the old fashioned way: we're going to use dried black-eyed peas.

Depending on your market, you can buy dried black-eyed peas two ways. You can buy them in a bag or you can buy them bulk. Either way, once you get them home, you will want to carefully go through them since they (like all legumes) often contain little stones. Do NOT use this recipe if you are using the canned variety of black-eyed peas—and please, no jokes about using the rock band called Black-Eyed Peas in this recipe!

Because we are using the dried black-eyed peas for this dish, they will need to be soaked for twenty-four hours. When I soak any dried beans (legumes), I always change the water out a few times. This is just a phobia for me, and it does not have to be done.

Ingredients

1 pound dried black-eyed peas, rinsed and picked clean
6 cups chicken stock
2 white onions, chopped
6 cloves garlic, chopped
1 red pepper, stemmed, seeded, and minced
2 bay leaves
1 tsp. salt
1 tsp. minced fresh thyme
1 tsp. minced fresh sage
1 tsp. ground black pepper

Steps

1. Place the black-eyed peas into a large bowl and add enough water to cover by a couple of inches. Let the beans soak overnight.

2. Drain the beans and discard the soaking liquid.

3. In a large saucepan over medium heat, combine all of the ingredients and bring to a boil.

4. Reduce the heat to a simmer and cook 90 minutes or until the black-eyed peas are tender. If the liquid gets too low, add water or more stock.

5. Remove the pan from the heat.
6. Spoon the Black-Eyed Peas onto a serving platter and enjoy.

Baked Hominy

(Serves 4)

If I were to be totally honest with you, I would share the fact that I do not like hominy. I am not a big fan of its texture and its flavor. I, however, am not from the South, so perhaps I just have not been blessed to acquire a taste for this bastardization of corn!

If, like me, you are not a fan of hominy, do not turn this page! I have good news! With this recipe, a casserole of sorts, you do not taste the hominy. Yes, this is indeed a happy day. I make this dish for my dad (who is from the South) and for people who like Southern food, and yes, I will partake in a serving or two because I love the flavor of freshly melted cheddar cheese.

For this dish, I would only use canned hominy, and in doing so, remember to rinse it under cold water. Depending on how the hominy was canned, you might find that it clumps together when you remove it from the can. This is quite natural. To unclump it, just crumble it apart with your fingers.

Ingredients

2 cups hominy (canned)
½ cup butter
2 cloves garlic, minced
1½ cups grated cheddar cheese
1 cup milk
4 eggs, beaten

Steps

1. Preheat your oven to 350°F.
2. Drain and rinse the hominy (if clumped, crumble it apart).
3. In a medium sauté pan, melt the butter over medium heat.
4. Into the pan, add the garlic and sauté 2 minutes.
5. Stir in the hominy, cheese, milk, and beaten eggs.
6. Spoon the mixture into a 2-quart oven-proof casserole dish.
7. Place into the oven and bake 45 minutes.
8. Remove from the oven and let cool slightly before serving.

Cheddar Casserole

(Serves 4)

If you are as much a fan of cheese as I am, then get ready for a delicious trip to food nirvana. I first had this wonderful side dish when I was living outside of Milwaukee, Wisconsin. Since the lovely state of Wisconsin is known as the Dairy State, I figured a cheese dish would be natural to order. They served this alongside some delicious slices of roast pork, and it made for a very memorable dinner.

The original recipe for this dish (as you will see below) calls for crumbled soda crackers. There have been times when I made this dish and, during the course of putting it together, realized I had no soda crackers. Being from San Francisco, I did what any native would do: I popped some sourdough French bread into the food processor and made breadcrumbs. It worked very well.

This is what is considered a layered casserole. This simply means that you have to construct this dish. Don't let this deter you from making Cheddar Casserole as the steps are very easy. You will want to use a very good quality cheddar cheese; it can either be the yellow (orange) variety or the natural white variety.

Ingredients

2 Tbs. butter

2 eggs

2 egg yolks

1 cup milk

2 cups grated cheddar cheese

1 cup crumbled soda crackers, divided

2 Tbs. minced parsley

1 Tbs. minced chives

Steps

1. Preheat your oven to 350°F. Lightly oil or butter a 1-quart casserole dish.
2. In a medium bowl, whisk the eggs and the egg yolks until smooth and creamy.
3. Whisk in the milk and cheddar cheese until well blended.
4. In a medium bowl, toss the crumbled soda crackers with the parsley and chives.
5. Sprinkle one third of the cracker crumbs in the bottom of the prepared casserole dish; then spoon in half of the cheese mixture.
6. Repeat Step 5 and then top the dish with the last of the cracker crumbs.
7. Place into the oven and bake 40 minutes.
8. Remove from the oven and let cool slightly before serving.

Cheese-Creamed Onions

(Serves 4)

Creamed onions are truly an American holiday staple. I can remember Thanksgivings and Christmases of my past where this dish was always on the table, and it didn't matter if the entrée was fowl, beef, lamb, or ham—there was a large dish of creamed onions. This dish, Cheese-Creamed Onions, takes the American classic and gives it a little whiz (not to be confused with Cheez Whiz).

The original creamed onions is a classic Southern dish, and in its original state, it is quite delicious. This version, with the addition of cheese, comes from the Midwest, and it is made even more robust with the addition of mushrooms. If you are not a fan of fungus, you can leave the 'shrooms out.

So, you might be wondering with bated breath, what kind of cheese should be used? Whichever you like, as long as it is a melting cheese. I often use cheddar but have also made it with Monterey Jack and have enjoyed it greatly with a Pepper Jack. I would not, however, use a hard cheese as it will crust more than it will melt.

Ingredients
½ pound small mushrooms, sliced
¼ cup flour
4 Tbs. butter
1½ cups milk
1 cup grated cheddar cheese, divided
1 tsp. minced thyme
⅛ tsp (pinch) cayenne pepper
36 pearl onions, peeled
¼ cup dried breadcrumbs

Steps
1. Preheat your oven to 425°F. Lightly butter or oil a 3-quart casserole dish.
2. Brush any viable dirt from the mushrooms and cut off any tough/woody stems. Slice the mushrooms.
3. In a medium saucepan, melt the butter over medium heat. Whisk in the flour until smooth. (Congratulations, you just made a roux!)
4. Whisk in the milk until smooth and keep whisking 5 minutes (it will thicken as you whisk).

5. Remove the pan from the heat and stir in ¾ cup cheese until it has melted.

6. Into the pan, stir the thyme, cayenne pepper, onions, and mushrooms.

7. Spoon the mixture into the prepared casserole dish and top with the remaining cheese.

8. Sprinkle the breadcrumbs over the cheese.

9. Place into the oven and bake 50 minutes.

10. Remove from the oven and let cool slightly before serving.

Cinnamon and Brown Sugar Sweet Potatoes

(Serves 4)

There is nothing wrong with a sweet side dish. Matter of fact, there is nothing wrong with a dish that is almost a dessert becoming a side dish. This is one of my favorite sides when I am serving an entrée like roasted fowl or pork. It is simple. It can be thrown together in a matter of minutes, and everyone will love it—and yes, it is a great way to get kids to eat a great food (sweet potato) that is loaded with beta carotene.

To answer the question you are thinking, yes, you can use yams instead of sweet potatoes for this dish. As you are well aware, if you have read the previous pages (see Sweet Potato Biscuits on page 18) of this cooking opus, there is a pretty big difference between yams and sweet potatoes. The rule of thumb for sweet potatoes: the brighter the flesh, the sweeter the potato.

For those thinking this is like a filling for Sweet Potato Pie (page 284), you are kind of right. Cinnamon and Brown Sugar Sweet Potatoes is a little thicker (think mashed potatoes), and this doesn't include eggs. The flavor is close with this dish being slightly richer and thicker.

Ingredients
3 sweet potatoes, peeled and cubed
1 Tbs. butter
2 Tbs. cream
1 Tbs. brown sugar
¼ tsp. ground cinnamon

Steps
1. Place the potatoes into a pot of boiling water and cook until fork tender.
2. Drain the potatoes and discard the cooking liquid.
3. Place the potatoes into a large bowl and mash with a potato masher. Do NOT use a food processor or you'll wind up with paste.
4. Stir in the butter, cream, brown sugar, and cinnamon.

5. Let the potatoes rest a few minutes for the flavors to blend.

6. Spoon into a serving bowl and enjoy.

Corn Pudding

(Serves 4)

Puddings! They are as American as . . . England. Yes, puddings, for the most part, are English in origin (puddings as we known them today), but they have also played a big part in America's culinary history. Corn Pudding came to America about the same time as the Pilgrims, although Native Americans have been making a version of Corn Pudding since they shucked their first ear.

Corn Pudding is a very rich side dish (as you can see from the ingredients). For true Corn Pudding, you want the only sweetness to come from the corn, and it is for this reason you want to use only a sweet variety of freshly shucked corn. You also want to remember to use the natural corn milk as it, too, is sweet. To get the corn milk, you take the back of the knife (non-sharp side) and scrape the just-cleaned cob. You will see a milky substance run down the cob; this is "corn milk."

I fully realize there are some people who like to substitute half-and-half or milk for cream. If you do that here, you will ruin the dish so DON'T DO IT! This is a pudding which is baked in a bain-marie. What is that? It is a fancy French term meaning you bake it in a pan that has water in it.

Ingredients

4 cups fresh sweet corn kernels, plus corn milk from cobs (see step 2)
1 Tbs. flour
½ tsp. salt
⅛ tsp. cayenne pepper
¼ tsp. ground nutmeg
2 eggs, beaten
1 cup cream
3 Tbs. butter, melted

Steps

1. Preheat your oven to 350°F. Lightly oil or butter a 1½-quart casserole dish.
2. With a sharp knife, slice down the corn cob to remove the kernels. Turn the knife over (to the blunt edge) and scrape the corn milk from the cobs. Do this in a large bowl.
3. In a large bowl, stir all the ingredients until well blended.
4. Spoon into the prepared casserole dish.

5. Add a few inches of water into a roasting pan large enough to hold the casserole dish.

6. Place the casserole dish into the roasting pan. Be careful not to let any water overflow into the casserole dish.

7. Place into the oven and bake 50 minutes.

8. Remove from the oven and let cool slightly before serving.

Creamed Corn

(Serves 4)

Here is a fun little experiment. Go into your pantry or a cupboard and remove a can of creamed corn. Open the can. Pour the can into a bowl. Now seriously, does that look like corn? Be honest; it looks like someone had an allergic reaction to corn and retched it back up. That is NOT Creamed Corn. That is gunk!

Creamed Corn is actually a very simple and delicious side dish for really any entrée. Since this is a dish with very few ingredients, it is very important for the flavors to be fresh and vibrant. The best (and only) corn to be used to make Creamed Corn is any sweet variety. This Creamed Corn was a staple of many diners across America because of its simplicity.

Once you shuck the corn (remove the kernels from the cob) you will then want to remove the naturally sweet corn milk. To do this, you take the blunt end of your knife (the non-sharp part) and scrape it down the cob. You will see a milky substance run down the cob. This is what is referred to as "corn milk." You always add this with the corn to any recipe. Yum!

Ingredients

6 ears of fresh sweet corn kernels, plus corn milk from cobs (see step 1)

¼ cup butter

¼ cup cream

Steps

1. With a sharp knife, slice down the corn cob to remove the kernels. Turn the knife over (to the blunt edge) and scrape the corn milk from the cobs. Do this in a large bowl.

2. In a medium sauté pan or skillet melt the butter over medium heat.

3. Stir in the corn and cook a few minutes.

4. Stir in the cream and cook 10 minutes, stirring the entire time.

5. Remove the pan from the heat and spoon into a serving bowl.

Creamed Peas and Potatoes

(Serves 4)

Depending on where you live in America, this is a classic holiday side dish. I have enjoyed it during various holidays in the South and Midwest. Out in the Southwest and Northwest, I don't think they have heard of this dish—unless of course they have migrated to these areas from regions that do prepare it.

For this dish, you will use red potatoes—but not just any red potatoes. You want to use the smaller variety, sometimes called fingerlings. If you can, get these small red potatoes from an organic dealer or a market with a large produce section. There is no need to peel them (but do make sure you scrub the skins clean). As far as peas are concerned, out here in San Francisco I very seldom (if at all) see fresh peas at the market. I do grow my own but when it isn't the season, I will use frozen sweet baby peas.

I should point out something rather interesting about this dish. I once had Creamed Peas and Potatoes encased in a French shell (think pot pie) and it was rather incredible and made for a perfect brunch while sitting on the terrace of a Napa winery.

Ingredients

2 pounds small red potatoes, peeled if
   not organic

1½ cups freshly hulled peas

¼ cup butter

¼ cup flour

2 cups milk

½ tsp. salt

¼ tsp. ground white pepper

¼ tsp. ground nutmeg

Steps

1. Into a pot of boiling water, add the potatoes and cook 20 minutes or until fork tender.

2. Drain the potatoes and discard the cooking liquid.

3. Into a steamer over medium heat, add the peas and steam 5 minutes.

4. Remove the peas from the steamer and place into a bowl of cold water. (If using frozen peas, disregard steps 3 and 4.)

5. In a medium saucepan, melt the butter over medium heat. Whisk in the flour until smooth. (You just made a roux!)

6. Whisk in the milk, salt, white pepper, and nutmeg until smooth.

7. Stir in the potatoes and peas and cook 5 minutes (it will thicken).

8. Spoon into a serving bowl and let cool slightly before serving.

Cowboy Beans

(Serves 6)

So, what really are Cowboy Beans? Good question! They are a morphing of pork-and-beans, chili, and baked beans, and yes, this really was a dish made by the cooks on the wagon trains. You can still find these Cowboy Beans served at many dude ranches throughout the West as well as diners and roadside eateries.

The bean used for Cowboy Beans is a bean that was very popular during the cowboy era of America. It is the pinto bean, which many say was introduced to the West via Mexico (and this is probably true). The pinto is a smaller variety of bean, thus it cooks quicker and is also much more flavorful.

You will need to start Cowboy Beans twenty-four hours before you turn on the heat because the beans need to be soaked before you can start the recipe. This version of Cowboy Beans does feature jalapeño peppers. If you are not a fan of peppers or spiciness, you can eliminate them.

Ingredients

2 cups dried pinto beans, rinsed and picked clean
4 cups cold water
1 cup chopped smoked ham
2 white onions, chopped
8-ounce can tomato sauce
2 jalapeño peppers, stemmed, seeded, and minced
¼ cup brown sugar
2 tsp. chili powder
1 tsp. salt
½ tsp. dry mustard

Steps

1. Place the beans in a large bowl of cold water and soak overnight.
2. Drain the beans and discard the soaking liquid.
3. In a medium saucepan over high heat, combine the beans and 4 cups cold water and bring to a boil.
4. Reduce the heat to a simmer, cover, and cook 90 minutes.
5. Drain the beans and reserve the cooking liquid.
6. Preheat your oven to 325°F.

7. Into a large casserole dish, stir the beans, ham, onions, 1 cup of the reserved cooking liquid, tomato sauce, jalapeño peppers, brown sugar, chili powder, salt, and dry mustard.

8. Cover the casserole dish and place into the oven and bake 1 hour.

9. Remove the cover and bake 45 additional minutes (if the liquid is low, add more of the reserved cooking liquid.

10. Remove the beans from the oven and enjoy.

··· **Note** ···

If you are going to be using ham hocks instead of smoked ham, just add the ham hocks to the beans for the entire cooking process. Remove the meat from the bones before adding to the casserole dish in step 7.

Dirty Rice

(Serves 4)

Dirty Rice! If you have ever watched a movie set in the South, then you have heard of Dirty Rice. What makes the rice dirty? Well . . . it is not dirt. It is the ingredients cooked with the rice, albeit they look nothing like dirt. So, why is it called Dirty Rice? No one knows, and there seems to never be an explanation when it comes to dishes from the South.

The origins of Dirty Rice are from the Creole region of Louisiana. The traditional Dirty Rice calls for the inclusion of chicken innards, including the liver and giblets. This is quite good; however, most people are not really into eating gut, so most adapted versions will have other pieces of meat such as sausage, like this version.

Dirty Rice is popular year around in the South and can always be found on a holiday table. When you get away from the South, Dirty Rice is also becoming a favorite holiday staple but under a different name . . . Rice Dressing.

Ingredients

1 cup long-grain rice
2 cups chicken stock
2 tsp. butter
2 tsp. corn oil
1 white onion, chopped
2 cloves garlic, minced
1 rib celery, chopped
½ green bell pepper, stemmed, seeded, and chopped
1 pound smoked sausage, casing removed and chopped
1 tsp. minced thyme
1 tsp. salt
½ tsp. ground black pepper
¼ tsp. cayenne pepper
2 Tbs. minced parsley

Steps

1. In a medium saucepan, combine the rice and chicken stock and bring to a boil.
2. Reduce the heat to low, cover, and cook 20 minutes.
3. Remove the rice from the heat and let sit 10 minutes.

4. In a large sauté pan or skillet, melt the butter in the corn oil over medium heat.

5. Add the onion, garlic, celery, and green bell pepper and sauté 5 minutes.

6. Stir in the sausage, thyme, salt, pepper, cayenne, and parsley and cook 10 minutes.

7. Stir in the rice, cover, and cook 5 minutes.

8. Remove the Dirty Rice to a serving bowl and enjoy.

Fried Green Tomatoes

(Serves 4)

No, you're not going to be eating a movie! What you will be eating, however, is a scrumptious buttermilk-drenched and fried unripe tomato. Seems strange, huh? Well, not if you're from the South, as this dish is the epitome of Southern cooking and may be the patron saint of the authentic Southern dinner table.

An interesting question may be, how did someone ever think to fry unripe tomatoes? Pretty good question. I can only assume that some tomato gardener with no patience wanted to taste the benefits of his/her garden before the tomatoes were a robust red and decided, "Well, I'll dip 'em in some buttermilk, coat 'em in cornmeal, and fry 'em—it's the Southern way!"

It might be hard to find green tomatoes in your market if you live a distance away from the South. The best way to remedy this problem is to grow your own and, luckily, they now have plants and seeds which can be cultivated in every area of America—even in foggy San Francisco!

Ingredients
4 green tomatoes
½ cup buttermilk
1 cup yellow cornmeal
1 tsp. salt
½ tsp. ground black pepper
3 Tbs. corn oil

Steps
1. Remove the stems from the tomatoes and cut into ¼-inch slices.
2. Pour the buttermilk into a shallow dish.
3. In a separate shallow dish, whisk the cornmeal, salt, and black pepper.
4. In a medium sauté pan or skillet, heat the oil over medium heat.
5. Dip the tomato slices into the buttermilk and then dredge (coat) them in the cornmeal.
6. Carefully place into the hot oil and fry until golden on both sides.
7. Remove from the pan and place on a paper towel–lined plate before serving.

Hushpuppies

(Makes about 18, depending on size)

The first time I had Hushpuppies was when I was around ten years of age. We were at my grandmother's house in Fort Smith, Arkansas. She said she was going to fix Hushpuppies; being a San Francisco kid, I looked at my mother and asked, "Why are we going to eat shoes?" Yes, outside of the South, Hushpuppies were a brand of footwear.

So, what are Hushpuppies? They are a classic Southern fried savory cornmeal. There are more variations of Hushpuppies than there are Bobbie-Jos in the South. They can be plain, just-fried buttermilk cornmeal, or they can be fancy by adding whatever it is that is close to molding in the refrigerator. My personal favorite Hushpuppies are found in this recipe since I think the onions and garlic are a great flavor with the cornmeal.

I have only had Hushpuppies made with yellow cornmeal, and I do believe this is the original way to prepare them. I have learned, however, that there are many parts of the South where white cornmeal is used. Whatever type of cornmeal you prefer (the recipe and steps will be the same), you owe it to yourself to indulge in some true Americana and make a batch of Hushpuppies.

Ingredients

2 cups yellow cornmeal
2 Tbs. flour
1 tsp. baking powder
1 tsp. salt
2 scallions (green onions), minced

4 cloves garlic, minced
½ tsp. ground black pepper
2 eggs, beaten
1 cup buttermilk
corn oil, for frying

Steps

1. In a large bowl, whisk the cornmeal, flour, baking powder, and salt.
2. Stir in the scallions, garlic, black pepper, eggs, and buttermilk. Set the bowl aside 5 minutes.
3. In a large skillet, heat enough oil (about 2 inches) to 350°F on a deep-fry thermometer.
4. Drop the batter into the oil by the tablespoon and fry until golden.
5. Remove to a paper towel–lined plate and let cool slightly before serving.

Indian Pudding

(Serves 4)

Whenever I make Indian Pudding, I always get asked the same question: "Is it really Indian Pudding?" Yes, it is a pudding originating with Native Americans based in the New England area of the United States. It is not a dish created by the Indians in India. Though this dish is from the New England area, recipes for a pudding of this ilk can be found in recipes from tribes all over America.

This section is on side dishes, meaning dishes you serve alongside the main course (entrée). I mention this because there will be some people who will scream and holler that Indian Pudding is a dessert. Yes, it can be served as a dessert since it is sweet, but in many eateries throughout America, it is served as a side dish, and this is how I usually present it.

Indian Pudding is a cornmeal pudding laced with dried fruits, naturally sweetened with molasses and sugar, with a touch of spiciness from ginger and cinnamon. I think it goes well with any roasted entrée, especially pork, and makes for a fine addition to the Thanksgiving and Christmas dinner table.

Ingredients

2½ cups milk, divided
⅓ cup yellow cornmeal
2 Tbs. butter
⅓ cup molasses
¼ cup sugar
½ tsp. ground ginger
½ tsp. ground cinnamon
2 eggs, beaten
½ cup chopped dried fruit

Steps

1. Preheat your oven to 325°F. Lightly oil or butter a 1-quart casserole dish.
2. In a medium saucepan over medium heat, stir together 1 cup milk, cornmeal, and butter until it is smooth and comes to a boil.
3. Reduce the heat and cook the cornmeal 5 minutes.
4. Remove the cornmeal from the heat.
5. Stir in the molasses, sugar, ginger, and cinnamon.

6. In a small bowl, whisk the remaining milk and eggs.

7. Stir the egg mixture and dried fruit into the cornmeal.

8. Spoon the mixture into the prepared casserole dish.

9. Place into the oven and bake 75 minutes.

10. Remove from the oven and let cool slightly before serving.

Lemon-Roasted Potatoes

(Serves 4)

When I was growing up in San Francisco, there were a few family-owned restaurants which served Lemon-Roasted Potatoes with their fish and pork dishes. I loved these, most times, more than the entrée they were served with. The fresh flavor of the lemons blended with the smoky saltiness of the bacon is a true joy for the mouth.

You can use any type of potato to make this dish. I prefer to use the red variety as I think the flesh of this potato bakes much better for a dish such as this. If the potatoes are organic, there is no need or reason to peel them. Simply scrub the skins and then slice the potatoes according to the recipe.

Roasting potatoes is an interesting lesson in agitation. You never really know how long a potato will take to become fork-tender. When you see a time for roasting potatoes, it is always approximate. To test the potato for tenderness, simply poke it with a fork. If it goes in easily, the potatoes are ready to eat.

Ingredients

1 pound bacon, cooked and chopped
   (reserve the rendered bacon fat)
1 pound red potatoes, thinly sliced
1 red onion, thinly sliced
1 lemon, grated zest only
1 Tbs. minced marjoram

Steps

1. Preheat your oven to 450°F.

2. In a medium skillet or sauté pan, stir 3 Tbs. of the rendered bacon fat, potatoes, onion, and lemon zest.

3. Place into the oven and roast for 20 minutes.

4. Stir in the bacon and marjoram and roast an additional 20 minutes.

5. Remove from the oven and let cool slightly before serving.

Smothered Onions

(Serves 6)

If you like onions, then you are going to love this dish which has its origins in the South and has been a favorite at roadside eateries for decades. It is the perfect accompaniment to pork chops or a roasted pork loin, and it is almost impossible to screw up.

If you order this dish in the South, it will always be made with sweet onions, as the South is known for their sweet onions, especially their famed Vidalia onions. When you head more westward, the dish is made with a typical yellow onion. If you do opt to use a regular yellow onion, you might want to add a tablespoon of brown sugar to the dish.

When I first had this dish at a diner in the South (with a couple of pork chops), I was taken aback by the flavor. Yes, it was oniony, but there was something else. I finally asked the cook, and he told me the secret to the dish was apple cider! Apple cider and onions? Yes! What a wonderful couple they do make.

Ingredients

6 cups thinly sliced sweet onions

5 Tbs. butter

5 Tbs. flour

2 cups chicken stock

½ cup apple cider

1 cup cream

1 tsp. salt

1 tsp. ground black pepper

¼ tsp. ground nutmeg

Steps

1. Place the onions into a large pot of boiling water and cook 10 minutes.

2. Drain the onions, discard the cooking liquid, and set them aside.

3. In a large sauté pan or skillet, melt the butter over low heat.

4. Add the flour to the butter and stir 5 minutes. (Congratulations, you just made a roux!)

5. Whisk in the chicken stock and apple cider until smooth and cook 5 minutes.

6. Add the onions and cream and cook 15 minutes.

7. Stir in the salt, black pepper, and nutmeg.

8. Spoon onto a serving platter and enjoy.

Oven-Roasted Garlic Potatoes

(Serves 4)

For me, Oven-Roasted Garlic Potatoes are a comfort food. If it was a Sunday in my house when I was growing up, there was going to be some kind of roast on the dinner table, and one of the side dishes was going to be Oven-Roasted Garlic Potatoes. This dish, in one form or another, has been a mainstay of the American kitchen for generations.

When it comes to roasting potatoes, I think red potatoes are the best, and the reason is simple: their texture holds up to the heat without getting mushy (as russets will). I have also made these with the popular gold potatoes (such as Yukon Gold) and was not too impressed. If the potatoes are organic, there is no need to peel them, but do remember to scrub the skins clean.

Garlic! Can you ever have too much garlic? You can play with the garlic here all you like. Add some, take some away, or even use elephant garlic (the giant garlic you might see at the market). It is the same with the herbs—use whichever herb you like—and I would use dried herbs over fresh when they are in a dish that will be roasted.

Ingredients

1 pound red potatoes, thinly sliced
6 cloves garlic, whole and unpeeled
2 Tbs. olive oil
1 tsp. dried rosemary
1 tsp. dried oregano
1 tsp. dried thyme

Steps

1. Preheat your oven to 450°F.
2. In a large baking dish, combine all of the ingredients.
3. Place into the oven and roast 45 minutes.
4. Remove from the oven and carefully squeeze out the garlic pulp from their skins.
5. Toss everything together, spoon onto a serving platter, and enjoy.

Potato and Onion Gratin

(Serves 4)

Ooooh look, a fancy French dish in an American cookbook. Well, yes, it is French in origin, but foods cooked in the au gratin fashion have been a staple of American cooking since the 1800s and perhaps even earlier.

When a particular food is cooked "au gratin," it simply means it is a dish which has been placed under a broiler (usually) so that its topping (usually cheese) has been crusted over. The word "gratin" loosely means "grated," as in the cheese—and there is today's culinary history lesson. Though this dish is often called a "gratin," it actually isn't because there isn't any cheese and it isn't placed under a broiler.

When made in many homes across America, this dish is usually prepared in a gratin dish, which is an elongated oven-proof dish with handles on both ends. When this dish was made in diners and other such eateries, it was done in a simple skillet or pan.

Ingredients

4 large russet potatoes, peeled and thinly sliced

2 yellow onions, chopped

4 cloves garlic, minced

1 egg, beaten

2 cups milk, heated to a simmer

2 Tbs. butter, chilled and diced

Steps

1. Preheat your oven to 375°F. Lightly oil or butter a large oval oven-proof gratin dish.

2. Layer the potatoes and onions into the gratin dish.

3. In a large bowl, whisk the garlic, egg, and milk until blended.

4. Pour the milk over the potatoes.

5. Dot the top of the gratin with the butter.

6. Place into the oven and bake 45 minutes or until the potatoes are fork-tender and the top is browning.

7. Remove from the oven and let cool slightly before serving.

Onion and Garlic Mashed Potatoes

(Serves 4)

I once had someone ask me, "What is the difference between mashed potatoes and smashed potatoes?" Well . . . the difference lies in which part of America you are living. Out here in the West, it is "mashed." When you start heading east, you'll get the people who prefer "smashed." No matter where you may be, however, the fact is mashed/smashed potatoes are one of the favorite dishes to hit the American table.

Let us talk mashed potatoes and not processed potatoes. Potatoes which you "mash" in a food processor become a paste. They lose all texture. They are something you should hang wallpaper with and not put into your body. Is it really too hard to use a potato masher? And then there are the lumps. There is nothing wrong with lumps in your mashed potatoes. This is called texture!

One of the things I like about Onion and Garlic Mashed Potatoes is that it contains three of my favorite foods: onions, garlic, and potatoes. You don't even need a gravy (although a gravy goes well with these). If you are of the ilk who thinks potatoes are boring, this dish will change your mind.

Ingredients

2 Tbs. butter
1 yellow onion, thinly sliced
4 cloves garlic, minced
4 large potatoes, peeled and diced
¼ cup half-and-half (may need more or less, depending on size of potatoes)
½ tsp. salt
¼ tsp. ground black pepper

Steps

1. In a medium skillet or sauté pan, melt the butter over medium heat.
2. Add the onions and sauté 5 minutes.
3. Add the garlic and sauté 5 minutes.
4. Remove the pan from the heat and set aside.
5. Place the potatoes into a large pot of boiling water and cook until fork-tender.

6. Drain the potatoes and discard the cooking liquid.
7. Using a potato masher, mash the potatoes.
8. Stir in the onion-garlic mixture, half-and-half, salt, and pepper.
9. Spoon into a serving bowl and enjoy.

Spiced Squash

(Serves 4)

I think the main reason why so many people do not like squash is because of the name "squash." It is too close to "squish." Change the name to something a little more artsy, and people will try it. Then again, if people like it too much, the price will go up, and those of us who love it will be screwed. Sort of a culinary conundrum.

The squash we are going to be using for Spiced Squash is an acorn squash, and this is readily available in all markets during the autumn and winter months. It is one of the small squash varieties (albeit not as small as zucchini or crookneck), and one half of an acorn squash can feed one or two people. It has a slightly sweet taste and is very easy to cook with.

When you buy your acorn squash for this dish, you want one that is about the size of a small ball (they are round). If you buy one that is too big, the flesh can be rather stringy and tough, and it will not bake well at all. By the way, if you are a fan of pumpkin, you can use small pumpkins for this dish as well.

Ingredients

2 acorn squash, halved and seeded
¼ cup butter
¼ cup honey
¼ cup brown sugar
½ tsp. ground cinnamon
¼ tsp. ground ginger
¼ tsp. ground mace
1 Tbs. lemon juice
¼ cup chopped pecans

Steps

1. Preheat your oven to 350°F.

2. Using a shallow baking pan, place the acorn squash skin-side down (which would mean the cut-side is facing up).

3. Add enough water into the pan so that it covers about a quarter of the squash's rind.

4. In a medium saucepan, melt the butter over medium heat.

5. Stir in the honey, brown sugar, cinnamon, ginger, mace, and lemon juice and cook until the brown sugar dissolves.

6. Spoon the mixture into the acorn squash halves.

7. Place the squash into the oven and bake 1 hour, basting with the honey mixture about every 15 minutes.

8. Remove the squash from the oven and sprinkle with the pecans.

9. Place back into the oven and bake an additional 10 minutes.

10. Remove the squash from the oven, place onto a serving platter, and enjoy.

From the Garden

Salads

Ambrosia

(Makes about 4 servings)

Ambrosia. Just saying the word sounds delicious. It just rolls off your tongue as smoothly as the food called Ambrosia slips down your gullet. Chances are most people have eaten a form of Ambrosia—and Lord knows, there are many forms out there—but what really is Ambrosia?

In the literal sense, Ambrosia was a food for longevity and immortality, eaten by the Greek gods, and it usually consisted of fruits and nuts. In today's world, Ambrosia is a fruit-based type of salad, which, according to lore, was created somewhere in the South. As far as what should actually be in an Ambrosia salad, there are no rules; to prove this, just Google "Ambrosia," and you will see a myriad of recipes.

In Hawaii, the paradise of America, they have their own version of Ambrosia, and to say I fell in love with it would be a gross understatement. As opposed to many other variations of Ambrosia, this contains no solid coconut. As a matter of fact, it only contains two solid ingredients, which are enveloped in a naturally sweet and exotic dressing.

Ingredients

4 oranges, peeled and sectioned
1 pineapple, skinned, cored, quartered, and thinly sliced
¼ cup coconut milk
2 Tbs. organic honey
¼ tsp. almond extract

Steps

1. In a large bowl, combine the oranges and pineapple.

2. In a medium bowl, whisk the coconut milk, honey, and almond extract.

3. Pour the dressing over the fruit and toss to coat.

4. Chill the Ambrosia at least 2 hours before serving.

Carrot Salad

(Serves 4)

In my way of thinking, there is nothing more refreshing on a warm summer or spring day than lounging on a patio and munching on a freshly made Carrot Salad. Not only is it delicious and healthy, almost everything in a Carrot Salad is a cancer fighter!

This recipe is for the all-time diner favorite Carrot Salad. It is very good, but there are some people who do not like celery in their Carrot Salad—and if you are such a person, might I recommend using parsnips instead? I had a Carrot Salad like this at a winery café in Sonoma, California, and it was tremendous—and no, I honestly did not miss the celery (even though I am a fan of celery).

For the best results in both taste and texture, I highly recommend using organic carrots. Their flavor is much more naturally sweet, and the vibrancy in their color makes the presentation of the salad much more attractive. If you're wondering if you can use the newer heirloom carrots (in various colors), yes, if you want to munch on a rainbow.

Ingredients

3 cups shredded carrots
1 cup minced celery (or shredded parsnips)
1 cup raisins
½ cup chopped walnuts
¾ cup mayonnaise
1 Tbs. brown sugar
½ tsp. ground nutmeg

Steps

1. In a large bowl, combine the carrots, celery, raisins, and walnuts.

2. In a medium bowl, whisk the mayonnaise, brown sugar, and nutmeg.

3. Pour the dressing over the carrots and toss to coat.

4. Let the Carrot Salad chill 2 hours before serving.

Black-Eyed Pea Salad

(Serves 6)

If it is a Sunday in the South or Midwest, then there will be a church picnic. If there is a church picnic, there will be tables laden with food, and two of those foods will always be fried chicken and black-eyed peas. If it is a very good Sunday and the church folks really love you, there will be a classic called Black-Eyed Pea Salad.

Black-eyed peas are a mainstay in the South and Midwest. As you begin to motor towards the West Coast, their popularity diminishes a little, and this is truly unfortunate as these little legumes are not only nutritional powerhouses, they are just downright delicious. For the sake of ease, we won't go into the full presentation of preparing dried black-eyed peas and will simply use the canned variety.

This salad is unlike the usual bean salad. It is a cornucopia of flavors and textures. It is best if you make it the day before you serve it, so all the flavors can blend perfectly. In the diners and cafés that feature this salad, they will often add leftover picnic or smoked ham. This is quite good, but if you are not into ham (or any meat), this is also an outstanding vegan/vegetarian dish as well.

Ingredients

2 cans black-eyes peas, drained and rinsed (or 2 cups prepared Black-Eyed Peas, see page 94)
1 sweet red bell pepper, seeded and minced
2 cups sweet corn kernels
½ pound bacon, cooked and chopped
¼ cup brown sugar
1 cinnamon stick
1 jalapeño pepper, seeded and minced
¼ cup water
¼ cup lime juice
2 Tbs. honey

Steps

1. In a large bowl, combine the black-eyed peas, red bell pepper, and corn kernels.
2. In a medium sauté pan or skillet over medium heat, combine the bacon, brown sugar, cinnamon stick, jalapeño pepper, water, lime juice, and honey. Bring to a boil.

3. Reduce the heat to a simmer and cook 10 minutes.
4. Spoon the bacon mixture into the beans and toss to coat.
5. Chill the salad at least 2 hours before serving.

Broccoli Salad

(Serves 4)

It wasn't that long ago when broccoli was one of the most hated vegetables in America. If you put broccoli on the table, it was considered a hate crime, and for all that is considered holy, never put it in front of a child. My, how times have changed. Now broccoli is beloved by millions, and kids are eating it raw!

Broccoli Salad used to be a regular feature in many diners across America. It was very cheap to make, and it took up space on the plate—two items which lead to profits. You don't see Broccoli Salad very often on diner menus anymore because the price has gone up dramatically. You will, however, see it on the menu at many of the chic cafés.

The secret to a great Broccoli Salad is two-fold. First, the broccoli should be blanched (briefly cooked in boiling water and then dipped in an ice bath). Secondly, it should be chopped and not served as florets—it's a salad dammit! By the way, do not leave out the peanuts when you make this. Their crunch and saltiness blend perfectly.

Ingredients

1 pound broccoli florets
2 scallions (green onions), minced
1 sweet red bell pepper, minced
½ cup salted peanuts (dry roasted are fine)
½ cup raisins
½ cup mayonnaise
2 Tbs. honey

Steps

1. Place the broccoli florets into a pot of boiling water and cook 5 minutes.
2. Remove the broccoli and place into a bowl of ice water. This will stop the cooking process.
3. Once cooled, coarsely chop the broccoli florets.
4. In a large bowl, combine the broccoli, scallions, red bell pepper, peanuts, and raisins.
5. In a medium bowl, whisk the mayonnaise and honey until smooth,
6. Spoon the dressing over the salad and toss to coat.
7. Chill the Broccoli Salad at least 2 hours before serving.

Creamy Peanut Coleslaw

(Serves 6)

Coleslaw has been a food mainstay in American diners, truck stops, roadside eateries, and virtually any place that sells food to eat since cabbage was first grown in a garden. Even people who don't like cabbage usually end up eating coleslaw. Why is coleslaw so popular? Because it goes with any and everything—whether it be a salad with a meal or the topping of a sandwich.

Every area in America has their favorite coleslaw. Perhaps even every city in America has their favorite coleslaw. This coleslaw is strictly Southern, and if you have ever heard the Southern adage "So good, you'll wanna slap your momma," you'll know what Creamy Peanut Coleslaw is all about.

The dressing for Creamy Peanut Coleslaw is unlike most other slaws. This is quite vibrant with a nice, subtle sweetness to it. It goes perfectly with the fresh taste of the cabbage and shredded carrots. As for the peanuts used in this coleslaw, any variety of salted peanut will work fine, including the dry-roasted varieties.

Ingredients

1 cup mayonnaise
¼ cup apple cider vinegar
¼ cup sugar
2 Tbs. milk
½ tsp. celery salt
1 head cabbage, cored and shredded
3 carrots, grated

4 scallions (green onions), chopped
¾ cup chopped salted peanuts

Steps

1. In a medium bowl, whisk the mayonnaise, apple cider vinegar, sugar, milk, and celery salt.

2. In a large bowl, toss together the cabbage, carrots, scallions, and peanuts.

3. Pour the dressing over the slaw and toss to coat.

4. Chill the Creamy Peanut Coleslaw at least 2 hours before serving.

Chopped Salad

(Serves 4)

Chop! Chop! Chop! Sometimes it seems that is all you do in the kitchen. True, it might be monotonous, but sometimes it can result in something healthy and delicious like this Chopped Salad. Actually when one thinks about it, this is a healthier version of the famed Cobb Salad sold in many of the finer upscale restaurants.

This version of a Chopped Salad comes from the West Coast and the Northwest. It is vegan and makes for not only a great dinner salad but also a wonderful vegan/vegetarian entrée salad. The ingredients listed are the basic ones for this salad, but as with most salads, you are free to play around with it. You just want to remember that whatever you add has to have the ability to be . . . chopped!

What I would not mess around with is the dressing for this salad. It is so refreshing, and the sweetness goes perfectly with the fresh vegetables. You can buy raspberry vinegar at any supermarket, and you will want a high quality virgin olive oil.

Ingredients

2 Tbs. raspberry vinegar

⅓ cup extra virgin olive oil

1 Tbs. organic honey

1 head butter lettuce, chopped

2 tomatoes, chopped

1 sweet red or yellow bell pepper, seeded and chopped

1 cucumber, peeled and chopped

1 red onion, chopped

Steps

1. In a small bowl, whisk the raspberry vinegar, olive oil, and honey.

2. In a large bowl, combine all of the chopped vegetables.

3. Spoon the dressing over the salad and toss to coat.

4. This salad is best served at room temperature, but if making ahead of time, chill it.

Diner Coleslaw

(Serves 6)

This is the most popular and common coleslaw which has been served in diners and eateries since about the time dinosaurs walked the earth. There is nothing fancy here. It is simply coleslaw the way it was meant to be made and served.

The history of coleslaw is rather interesting. The first known recipe of this favorite cabbage salad was recorded in 1770 in a Dutch cookbook, and it basically was this recipe right here. Throughout time, coleslaw has become an international favorite, with some even featuring meat in the slaw. Many of the American versions of coleslaw which feature carrots are of the British variety.

Due to the fact that most coleslaws feature mayonnaise, it is always a good idea to keep them chilled until ready to use. If you take coleslaw on a picnic (and many do), keep it in the ice chest or set the bowl in a larger bowl of shaved or chipped ice.

Ingredients

1 head cabbage, cored and
   shredded
⅔ cup mayonnaise
1 Tbs. heavy cream
½ tsp. salt
1 tsp. sugar
¼ tsp. ground black pepper

Steps

1. Place the shredded cabbage into a large bowl.

2. In a medium bowl, whisk the mayonnaise, heavy cream, salt, sugar, and pepper until smooth.

3. Pour the dressing over the cabbage and toss to coat.

4. Chill the Diner Coleslaw at least 2 hours before serving.

Diner Style Chicken Salad

(Serves 4)

Somewhere along the course of time, salads such as this Diner Style Chicken Salad and others featuring meat became ingredients for sandwiches. Though there is nothing wrong with slapping some of this tasty goodness between two slices of bread, the fact of the matter is they are salads and should be presented as thus!

I love salads such as these because they are a great way to make an entirely new dish from leftovers. This is the very same reason they became so popular during the heyday of diners across America. To make this salad, you can use any type of leftover chicken. It could have been baked, fried, roasted or broiled—it doesn't matter. You simply remove the skin and chop the meat.

The classic way to serve this salad is over a few leaves of crunchy iceberg lettuce. Nowadays, the chic cafés are serving it over beds of heirloom greens or baby spinach leaves. Either way is fine and perfect for a brunch with some freshly made bread and perhaps a glass of chilled white wine (or two).

Ingredients

1 cup mayonnaise

½ cup sour cream

1 stalk celery, minced

2 scallions (green onions), minced

1 cup chopped pecans

3 cups chopped cooked chicken
(white meat, dark meat, or combo)

12 seedless red grapes, halved

Steps

1. In a large bowl, whisk the mayonnaise and sour cream until smooth.

2. Add all the remaining ingredients and gently stir to combine.

3. Serve on leaves of iceberg lettuce.

Fruit Salad

(Serves 4)

Remember going into diners or other such eateries, and in the area behind the counter, they had plates of Fruit Salad sitting on ice? Fruit Salad has always been popular because it was refreshing, naturally sweet, filling, and healthy. Nowadays, the Fruit Salad is a little different but just as popular, if not more so, than in days of yore.

I guess you can say this version of a Fruit Salad is very California since I have had it many times while traversing the Golden State. I love the combination of fresh fruit, and the honey and lime juice dressing is a perfect accompaniment. You can use any melon for this salad, but I would tend to stay away from watermelon for the simple reason that its juices will dilute the dressing, thus taking away from the overall freshness of the dish.

Of course, it should go without saying (but I will anyway) that any fruit salad is subject to the season. Don't try to cheat by using frozen or canned fruit; it is not the same thing. Just use your imagination and conjure up a Fruit Salad to fit the season!

Ingredients

1 cantaloupe, seeded and cubed
1 honeydew, seeded and cubed
1 cup seedless red grapes
1 cup blueberries
2 peaches, peeled, pitted, and sliced
2 bananas, peeled and sliced
⅓ cup organic honey
1 lime, juice and finely grated zest

Steps

1. In a large bowl, combine all the fruit and gently toss.
2. In a small bowl, whisk the honey, lime juice, and zest.
3. Pour the dressing over the fruit and gently toss to coat.
4. Chill the salad before serving.

Roast Potato Salad

(Serves 4)

Nope, this is not your mother's potato salad. No way is this the after-church-picnic potato salad. You will never see this potato salad at your local deli. This is a new wave American potato salad which is becoming quite popular out here in the West. And you want to know something? It is downright delicious!

The fact of the matter is the original potato salads were never gunky. They never had mayonnaise in them. They were a way to present potatoes in which you actually got to taste the potatoes. This is not only a wonderful salad; it is also a great side dish.

The best potatoes to use for this dish are red potatoes, and if they are organic, then there is no need to peel them. You will want to use fresh herbs for this dish as they will be added to the salad after the potatoes have been roasted. This will give you the freshest taste possible.

Ingredients

1½ pounds red potatoes, cubed
2 Tbs. corn oil
1½ Tbs. red wine vinegar
1 tsp. Dijon-style mustard
2 Tbs. olive oil
½ red onion, minced
2 tsp. minced parsley
2 tsp. minced chives
1 tsp. minced thyme
1 tsp. minced rosemary
¼ pound bacon, cooked and minced

Steps

1. Preheat your oven to 450°F.

2. In a medium roasting pan, add the potatoes and corn oil and toss to coat them.

3. Place into the oven and roast 40 minutes.

4. In a small bowl, whisk the vinegar, mustard, and olive oil. Set the bowl aside.

5. Remove the potatoes and place them in a large serving bowl. Spoon the dressing over the potatoes and toss them to coat.

6. Sprinkle the onion, minced herbs, and bacon over the potatoes and gently toss before serving.

··· **Note** ···

If you use any other type of potato, the cooking time will be different.

Roasted Corn Salad

(Serves 6)

One of the great joys about the dawn of any summer is the fact that freshly harvested corn will soon be making its way into the produce section of the supermarkets. Fresh corn and summer are one of nature's great marriages. Once the corn hits the markets and the grills come out to play, Americans love their roasted corn, and if you're really lucky, you'll get someone to make a refreshing Roasted Corn Salad!

Roasted Corn Salad is becoming quite popular at barbecue eateries and for good reason. Aside from being almost addictive, it goes well with any grilled dish. The best way to roast (or grill) corn is the simplest. Pull the husk down the corn to the stem and then remove the corn silk (the stringy fibers). Bring the husks back up to the top and tie them closed with some kitchen twine. Soak the cobs in cold water for about an hour. Place them under the broiler or on the grill until the husks char. Remove them, let them cool, strip off the husks, and you have perfect grilled or roasted corn!

The dressing for this Roasted Corn Salad is not as acidic as most as you don't want the dressing interfering with the freshness of the roasted corn or its natural sweetness. The dressing does have a little spicy snap to it due to the inclusion of the jalapeño peppers, but if you want, you can always omit them from the recipe.

Ingredients

6 ears corn, roasted (see note above)
1 tomato, chopped
1 rib celery, minced
2 Tbs. minced cilantro
½ red onion, minced
¼ cup olive oil
1 Tbs. apple cider vinegar
2 jalapeño peppers, stemmed, seeded, and minced
2 tsp. lime juice
1 tsp. salt

Steps

1. With a sharp knife, remove the roasted corn kernels from the cobs and place into a large bowl.
2. Add the tomato, celery, cilantro, and onion and toss together.

3. In a medium bowl, whisk the olive oil, vinegar, jalapeño peppers, lime juice, and salt.

4. Pour the dressing over the salad and toss to coat.

5. Let the Roasted Corn Salad sit at room temperature 30 minutes before serving.

Red Cabbage and Apples

(Serves 4)

Once you look at this recipe, you might say to yourself, "Isn't this a coleslaw?" If you were going to say that loosely, I suppose it can be considered a coleslaw, but there is one ingredient in this dish which you will never find in a coleslaw, and that ingredient is . . . wine!

Cabbage and apples have been a partner in food for quite some time. The natural sweetness of the apples blends very well with the freshness of the cabbage, and both textures complement each other perfectly. With this in mind, it is only logical that someone would come up with a salad featuring the two.

This salad is quite different from most other salads in so much that it is cooked. This is not a salad you make right out of the refrigerator. This type of salad is becoming quite popular at cafés throughout the West Coast, and I think it is a nice and delicious change.

Ingredients

2 Tbs. butter
1 head red cabbage, cored and shredded
2 Granny Smith apples, cored, peeled, and thinly sliced
2 Tbs. sugar
¼ cup dry white wine
¼ cup chicken stock
1 tsp. salt

Steps

1. In a large sauté pan, melt the butter over medium heat.
2. Add the cabbage and sauté 5 minutes.
3. Stir in the remaining ingredients and cook 10 minutes.
4. Remove the pan from the heat.
5. Spoon the Red Cabbage and Apples to a serving platter and enjoy.

Smoked Ham Salad

(Serves 4)

Like the recipe we shared for Diner Style Chicken Salad (page 132), this is another "salad" which has been bastardized into a sandwich spread. Smoked Ham Salad was created as a way to use leftover ham and was always quite popular after any holiday which featured ham as the meal. If the leftover ham was not being used to make a soup, it was being used to make this incredibly tasty salad. By the way, please do not confuse this with that stuff in a can called "deviled ham."

You can use any type of ham to make this dish, but I think the best is always leftover picnic ham. The texture and the sweet-salty flavor of the picnic ham is simply perfection. To properly present this Smoked Ham Salad as it was at diners long ago, you simply spoon some over leaves of iceberg lettuce. If you want to make this for a brunch, a nice little treat is to serve it with thinly sliced toasted baguettes.

On a side note, I did have a salad like this prepared with bacon instead of the ham. I found it interesting and flavorful but kind of weird to eat. If you want to try it that way while the bacon rage continues on, I would recommend frying the bacon just until it is chewy and not too crisp.

Ingredients

1 pound smoked ham, minced
2 ribs celery, minced
2 scallions (green onions), minced
4 sweet pickles, minced
½ tsp. ground black pepper
1 Tbs. yellow mustard
½ cup mayonnaise

Steps

1. In a large bowl, combine the ham, celery, scallions, and sweet pickles.
2. In a small bowl, whisk the black pepper, mustard, and mayonnaise until smooth.
3. Spoon the dressing over the ham and stir to mix.
4. Serve over leaves of iceberg lettuce.

Sweet Potato Salad

(Serves 4)

This salad has been around much longer than the current "raw food" fad. What is "raw food"? Simply put, it is food which is served in its natural state—not cooked. This Sweet Potato Salad is a popular café salad in many eateries throughout Northern California, and it is quite refreshing and tasty.

What we are going to do here you might find strange. We are going to eat raw (uncooked) sweet potatoes. I think you'll be surprised at just how good they are! When you eat raw sweet potatoes, you will be tasting the sweet side of Mother Nature in all of her glory. The texture will be much like grated carrot for a carrot salad.

For the best possible flavor combination, I would recommend using Granny Smith apples for this salad. They have a tart sweetness to them, and they marry well with the sweet potatoes. If you don't like pecans or can't afford them, you can use any other type of "soft" nut such as walnuts—or as I often do, roasted pumpkin seeds. By the way, when grating the sweet potatoes you might want to wear gloves as, depending on the potato, they can turn your hands orange.

Ingredients

1 cup grated sweet potatoes
2 cups diced apples
½ cup chopped pecans
¾ cup raisins
½ cup chopped celery
6 Tbs. mayonnaise

Steps

1. Place all of the ingredients into a large bowl and gently toss to coat.
2. Chill at least 2 hours before serving.

Three Bean Salad

(Serves 4)

Wow, talk about a classic American salad! I don't think you can get more classic than the old standby for any party or picnic: the famed Three Bean Salad. For something so simple, it is so delicious. This recipe is for the classic Three Bean Salad you may have enjoyed at diners, truck stops, and other roadside eateries.

One of the great things about Three Bean Salad is that you can let your mind go crazy with combinations of beans. I have had a Southwest version featuring black and pinto beans. I have had a Southern version with black-eyed peas and lima beans. It is a fun dish to play with, but my all-time favorite is still this classic version with kidney, garbanzo, and wax beans (a yellow version of green beans).

When using canned beans, always remember to drain and rinse them under cold running water. The dressing here might be a little too acidic for some. If this is the case, you can use a cider vinegar or just cut down on the red wine vinegar.

Ingredients

15-ounce can kidney beans, drained and rinsed

15-ounce can garbanzo beans, drained and rinsed

15-ounce can wax beans, drained and rinsed

3 scallions (green onions), minced

4 cloves garlic, minced

¼ cup olive oil

3 Tbs. red wine vinegar

½ tsp. salt

1 tsp. yellow mustard

Steps

1. In a large bowl, combine all of the beans, scallions, and garlic.

2. In a small bowl, whisk the olive oil, vinegar, salt, and mustard.

3. Pour the dressing over the beans and toss to coat.

4. Chill at least 2 hours before serving.

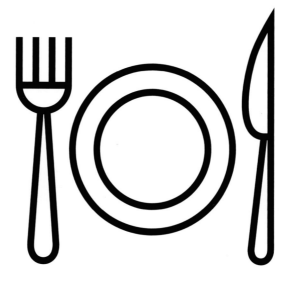

Blue Plate Specials

Entrees

Apple Whiskey Chops

(Serves 4)

Whenever I even think about pork chops, I begin to salivate. For many of us, pork chops are one of the ultimate comfort foods. When I was growing up, we had pork chops a few times a week, albeit we never had Apple Whiskey Pork Chops, but close . . . my mom always made applesauce to go along with them.

This is almost a one-pot meal because, along with cooking the pork chops, you will be making a side dish with the apples. Think of it as applesauce without the apples being "sauced" and with the zip of some good old-fashioned American whiskey (or bourbon, if you prefer). While on the subject of bourbon or whiskey, it is not true that all alcohol burns off when it is cooked, so be advised should you be preparing this dish for anyone with an alcohol-related illness.

The best apples to use for this dish are the tart green Granny Smith apples. Their flavor will blend well with the whiskey or bourbon and they will accentuate the natural flavor of the pork chops as long as you only season them with salt and pepper.

Ingredients

4 pork chops, any thickness
salt and pepper to taste
1 Tbs. corn oil
3 Granny Smith apples, peeled, cored, and quartered
½ cup whiskey or bourbon

Steps

1. Season the pork chops with salt and pepper.

2. In a medium skillet, heat the oil over medium-high heat.

3. Place the pork chops in the skillet and fry 5 minutes per side (or to desired doneness). Remove the pork chops and set aside.

4. Into the skillet, add the apples and cook until they begin to caramelize (brown). Remove the apples and set aside.

5. Remove the skillet from the heat and stir in the whiskey.

6. Place the skillet back onto the heat, bring the whiskey to a boil, and cook 2 minutes.

7. Place the pork chops and apples back into the skillet.

8. Partially cover the skillet and cook 10 minutes.
9. Remove the pork chops and apples and place them onto a serving platter.
10. Increase the heat to high and cook the liquid until it becomes a syrup (thickened).
11. Spoon the sauce over the pork chops and enjoy.

BBQ Sauce Meatloaf

(Serves 4)

Meatloaf: The one word that can make some people shudder, make some people run from the dinner table, and, for true "meatloafobic" people, cause projectile vomiting in the dining room. Yep, I used to be one of those people, but now, depending on the meatloaf, I will be the first one to sit down at the table.

In this section on Blue Plate Specials, I will be sharing with you some of my favorite meatloaf recipes. Meatloaf, as we know it, is truly American (albeit the idea is French in origin, and it is technically a pâté) and has been a staple in diners, truck stops, cafés, and roadside eateries since the first flame met a burner. They are a humble dish and, when prepared properly, quite delicious, and the leftovers make for one of the best sandwiches in the known world.

This meatloaf has a combination of ground beef and ground pork, thus it will be rather moist and rich in flavor. Aside from the freshness of the vegetables within the meatloaf, it also has the added flavor of having barbecue sauce baked atop it during its final stage in the oven. A point to remember when cooking a meatloaf: it is very natural for them to shrink during the cooking process.

Ingredients

1 Tbs. corn oil
1 small yellow onion, minced
½ sweet red bell pepper, seeded and minced
3 cloves garlic, minced
1 tsp. ground black pepper
1 tsp. chili powder

1 tsp. celery salt
½ tsp. ground cumin
1¼ pounds ground beef
¾ pound ground pork
½ cup rolled oats
1 egg, beaten
¼ cup quality barbecue sauce

Steps

1. Preheat your oven to 350°F. Line the bottom of a 9x5-inch loaf pan with parchment paper.

2. In a medium sauté pan, heat the oil over medium heat.

3. Add the onion, bell pepper, and garlic and sauté 5 minutes.

4. In a large bowl, combine the pepper, chili powder, celery salt, cumin, ground beef, ground pork, rolled oats, egg, and sautéed onion mixture.

5. Using your hands, mix everything together until very well combined. Yes, it gets messy, but it's fun.

6. Spoon the mixture into the prepared loaf pan.

7. Place into the oven and bake 75 minutes or until it reaches 165°F on a meat thermometer.

8. Pour the barbecue sauce over the meatloaf.

9. Place back into the oven and bake 15 additional minutes.

10. Remove from the oven and let cool slightly before slicing and serving.

··· Note ···

For any meatloaf, to ascertain if it is done, check the internal temperature with a meat thermometer. To be safe for consumption, it must read at least 160°F.

Beef and Pork Meatloaf

(Serves 4)

This is the mindset of a diner or roadside eatery cook: "I have a little leftover ground beef from last night's menu and a little leftover sausage from this morning's breakfast, so I'll blend them together and make a meatloaf." Unbeknownst to themselves, they were economic geniuses: they saved money and increased profits—the two most important elements of running a successful eatery.

This is the meatloaf you might remember as a kid if you ever ordered it at a diner. It is ground beef (as usual), and instead of blending it with normal ground pork, it is blended with ground pork sausage meat. The flavor is quite nice, and I think this meatloaf makes one of the best sandwiches.

When it comes to the ground pork sausage meat, you do not have to grind your own. You can use the store-bought variety of ground sausage, or if you have a butcher, you can buy it in bulk (meaning, by the pound and freshly ground). Both of these types of ground sausage meat have added herbs and spices, and this will pose no problem.

Ingredients

2 pounds ground beef
½ pound ground pork sausage meat
1 egg, beaten
2 cups minced scallions (green onions)
½ cup rolled oats
2 Tbs. Worcestershire sauce
1 cup ketchup, divided

Steps

1. Preheat your oven to 350°F. Line the bottom of a 9x5-inch loaf pan with parchment paper.

2. In a large bowl, combine the ground meats, egg, scallions, rolled oats, Worcestershire sauce, and ¾ cup ketchup. Mix thoroughly with your hands. Yes, it is messy, but it is fun too.

3. Spoon the mixture into the prepared pan.

4. Place the meatloaf into the oven and bake 45 minutes.

5. Remove from the oven and spoon the remaining ketchup atop.

6. Place back into the oven and bake 45 additional minutes.

7. Remove the meatloaf from the oven and let cool in the pan.
8. Remove the meatloaf from the pan onto a serving plate.
9. Carve the meatloaf and serve.

Beef Brisket

(Serves 4)

Beef brisket is a cut of meat that is currently very popular among grillers and smokers. It is a much-marbled piece of meat and, when prepared properly, is simply delicious. If you are not familiar with a beef brisket, let me remind you that if you have ever had corned beef, you have had beef brisket. Corned beef is salt-cured beef brisket.

This was prepared in the eateries throughout America much like a pot roast. It was slow roasted with vegetables and a combination of stock and wine, which gives it an incredible gravy. It was then served over wide egg noodles or over mashed potatoes (depending on which part of the country you were dining). It is simply scrumptious.

There will be arguments regarding whether you should trim or not trim the fat from the brisket for this dish. I always trim the fat. Due to the length of the cooking, it will still be quite tender, and I won't have to skim the fat during the cooking process. It should be noted that the brisket does need a twenty-four hour marinating period.

Ingredients

4 cloves garlic, minced
2 tsp. salt
2 tsp. ground black pepper
2 tsp. ground paprika
3-pound beef brisket, trimmed of excess fat
¼ cup dry red wine
2 Tbs. Worcestershire sauce
2 cups beef stock
1 yellow onion, sliced
1 orange, peeled and sectioned
4 red potatoes, peeled and diced
2 carrots, diced
2 parsnips, diced

Steps

1. In a small bowl, stir together the garlic, salt, pepper, and paprika.
2. Rub the garlic mixture all over the beef brisket. Wrap the brisket in plastic and chill overnight.
3. Preheat your oven to 350°F.

4. Heat a large sauté pan or skillet over medium-high heat.
5. Place the beef brisket in the pan and brown on all sides.
6. Remove the pan from the heat.
7. Pour the wine, Worcestershire sauce, and beef stock over the beef brisket.
8. Add the onions and orange and place a lid on the pan.
9. Place into the oven and roast 2 hours.
10. Add the potatoes, carrots, and parsnips.
11. Place back into the oven, without a lid, and roast 60 minutes.
12. Remove from the oven and place the beef on a serving platter surrounded by the vegetables.
13. Spoon the sauce over the dish and enjoy.

Buttermilk Baked Chicken

(Serves 4)

You aren't going to get much more Southern than this dish, except maybe for some different fried chicken dishes. In making this dish, you are going to prepare the baking pan in a true Southern way. While you are preparing the ingredients, you will be preheating not just the oven, but the pan as well. I have only seen Southerners do this, and it must mean something because you won't find too many Southern dishes that don't taste good.

Whenever I am asked to describe this dish, I always refer to it as a "poor man's casserole." The reason I use this term is because it is prepared like a casserole yet without many ingredients. This is Southern simplicity. My favorite way to serve this dish is with some buttermilk biscuits, as the biscuits will soak up all the yummy gravy.

This recipe does call for Cream of Mushroom Soup. Now, you can make your own Cream of Mushroom Soup (you will find my recipe on page 70), or you can do what the diners, cafés, and roadside eateries do and use a good quality canned variety—just make sure it is low in sodium (salt).

Ingredients

¼ cup butter
4 chicken breasts, with breast bone and skin intact
½ tsp. salt
¼ tsp. ground black pepper
1½ cups buttermilk, divided
¾ cup flour
10¾-ounce can Cream of Mushroom Soup (or homemade, see page 70)

Steps

1. Preheat your oven to 425°F.
2. Place the butter in a large baking dish and place it in the oven while the oven is preheating.
3. Season the chicken with the salt and pepper.
4. Place the chicken in a shallow bowl.
5. Pour the ½ cup buttermilk over the chicken and turn a few times to coat.
6. Place the flour in a large ziplock bag.
7. Remove the chicken from the buttermilk and place into the flour. Shake the bag to dredge (coat) the chicken.

8. Place the chicken in the preheated baking dish, skin-side down, place back into the oven, and bake 25 minutes.

9. Turn the chicken over and bake 10 more minutes.

10. In a medium bowl, whisk the remaining buttermilk and the Cream of Mushroom Soup.

11. Pour the soup mixture over the chicken and bake 15 additional minutes.

12. Remove the Buttermilk Baked Chicken from the oven and let cool slightly before serving.

Cajun Pork Roast

(Serves 4)

My introduction to Cajun cooking was being taught by the late Paul Prudhomme. The man was one of the most incredible chefs I have ever known whose smile would radiate and whose love for Cajun cooking knew no end. He will forever be missed, and each time I make this Cajun Pork Roast, I think of him—and more often than not, a tear or two will fall.

When it comes to the actual piece of meat to make a pork roast, you have two basic options. First, you can buy what is referred to as a "pork roast." It is a good piece of meat, and rather obviously, it roasts well. Second, you can do what I do. I buy a whole pork tenderloin (they are pretty big) and cut my roasts from it. The pork tenderloin has less fat on it, and the meat is much more tender. Either way, this dish will come out perfect.

The spices used in Cajun cooking are just incredible. Not only do they taste good, but the aromas that will be wafting through your kitchen are droolworthy. The spices used for Cajun Pork Roast are blended to make a paste with the olive oil, and this paste is rubbed on the pork roast. There is no need to marinate this pork roast. Once it has been seasoned, plop that piggy in the oven.

Ingredients

2-pound pork roast
2 Tbs. olive oil
1 Tbs. chili powder
4 cloves garlic, minced
1 Tbs. dried oregano, crumbled
2 Tbs. dried thyme, crumbled
½ tsp. salt
½ tsp. ground black pepper
½ tsp. ground cumin

Steps

1. Preheat your oven to 350°F.

2. Place the pork roast into a roasting pan and rub it all over with the olive oil.

3. In a small bowl, whisk the chili powder, garlic, oregano, thyme, salt, pepper, and cumin.

4. Rub the spice mixture over the pork. As it meets the olive oil, it will become paste-like (this is what you want).

5. Place into oven and roast 1 hour or until 160°F on a meat thermometer.

6. Remove from the oven and let rest 10 minutes.

7. Slice thinly and enjoy.

Cajun Meatloaf

(Serves 4)

When I die, if it is at all possible, this is the meatloaf I want to take to the next world with me. This is an adaptation of the late Chef Paul Prudhomme's Cajun Meatloaf. It is beyond belief. The flavors here marry to absolute perfection, and interestingly enough, there is only one type of ground meat used—and that is ground beef.

While you are preparing this meatloaf, you are going to do something rather strange. During the process of mixing the ingredients by hand, you are going to be adding a hot (as in heat, not spice) ingredient. This can be dangerous, so as not to burn yourself, you might want to wear rubber gloves when mixing this. It is important to the texture and taste to mix this when hot, so no shortcuts are recommended. By the way, this is a formed meatloaf; no loaf pan is needed (unless you want to cheat).

When it comes to ground beef for a dish like this meatloaf, you do not want it to be too lean. You want the fat. It gives flavor and makes the meatloaf moist. You can always grind your own beef, giving you more control of the fat, but chances are, you won't. So, when you're at the market, you will want a 70/30 ground beef (30% fat). Yes, you can use 80/20, but it won't be as good.

Ingredients

1½ tsp. salt
1½ tsp. ground black pepper
1½ tsp. ground cayenne
½ tsp. ground cumin
½ tsp. ground nutmeg
1 bay leaf, crumbled
¼ cup butter
1 yellow onion, chopped

1 sweet green bell pepper, cored, seeded, and chopped
5 cloves garlic, minced
1 Tbs. hot pepper sauce
1 Tbs. Worcestershire sauce
½ cup milk
½ cup ketchup
2 pounds ground beef
1 egg, beaten

Steps

1. Preheat your oven to 350°F.
2. In a medium bowl, whisk the salt, pepper, cayenne, cumin, nutmeg, and bay leaf.
3. In a medium sauté pan or skillet, melt the butter over medium heat.
4. Add the onion and sauté 5 minutes.

5. Add the bell pepper and garlic and sauté 5 minutes.

6. Stir in the hot pepper sauce, Worcestershire sauce, and spice mixture. Keep stirring until thickened.

7. Stir in the milk and ketchup and bring to a boil.

8. Remove the pan from the heat.

9. In a large bowl, mix together the ground beef and the egg.

10. Add the hot mixture from the pan and, using your hands, mix thoroughly.

11. Shape into a meatloaf and place into a roasting pan.

12. Place into the oven and bake 30 minutes.

13. Place a foil tent over the meatloaf and bake an additional 40 minutes or until it reaches 160°F on a meat thermometer (the actual cooking time will depend on the thickness of the meatloaf).

14. Remove from the oven and let rest 10 minutes before slicing and serving.

Beer-Battered Fish Fry

(Serves 4)

When I had the pleasure of living in Wisconsin, I was surprised to find that, every Friday night, all the restaurants had the same menu: Friday Night Fish Fry. It didn't matter if it was an Asian restaurant, Italian, or French—if it was Friday night, they were frying fish. I later found out this was quite popular in many areas of America, and I am very cool with this because I happen to love a good Beer-Battered Fish Fry!

When it comes to frying fish in a batter, you want a fleshy type of fish. I like to use catfish, pollock, or halibut. If the fish isn't fleshy, then it may very well fall apart while it is being fried, and that is not a good thing. Also of great importance when frying fish (or frying anything really) is to have a good quality deep-fry thermometer. The temperature of the oil is important not only for the proper cooking of the fish but also for health reasons. If the temperature is too low, the oil will get into the batter, and you'll have a greasy fried fish. When the oil temperature is perfect, the minute the battered fish hits the oil, the batter hardens and the oil does not get into it.

Beer! What kind of beer is best for the batter? Well, when I was in Wisconsin, I am sure they only used Miller®. I use whatever beer I have on hand, which is usually a foreign beer with more hops. You can use any beer or ale.

Ingredients

1 cup flour
3 Tbs. paprika
2 tsp. salt
12-ounce bottle beer

2 tsp. yellow mustard
2 pounds fleshy fish fillets
vegetable oil for frying

Steps

1. In a large bowl, whisk the flour, paprika, and salt.
2. Stir in the beer and mustard to form a batter.
3. Over medium heat, bring 4 inches of oil to 350°F on a deep-fry thermometer.
4. Dip the fish into the batter and completely coat.
5. Carefully place into the hot oil and fry until golden.
6. Remove the fish to a paper towel–lined plate.
7. Let the fish cool slightly before serving.

Fritos®, Chili, and Cheddar Pie

(Serves 4)

Whenever I eat this dish, I harken back to my elementary school days. They actually made this in the cafeteria! It really is a rather cheeky dish, but it is also pure Americana. This is a great dish to use day-old chili or even something fun to make with canned chili. And yes, the Fritos in the title are indeed the very same Fritos corn chips.

Though this dish only contains four ingredients, it is a dish which needs to be layered in order to be served properly. This will be no problem as the layering process is very easy. This is one of those dishes which may be categorized as either a one-pot-meal or a casserole, both of which are very American. It is also a perfect dish to make for dinner after a hectic day when you don't want to spend hours over a hot burner.

The question for this dish has always been: Do you crumble the Fritos or not? It is a good question, of which there is no right or wrong answer. I have made it both ways, and it comes out tasting the same. You do want to serve this warm as it is really yummy when the cheese is gooey and melted.

Ingredients
3 cups Fritos corn chips, divided
1 cup chopped sweet onions, divided
2 cups grated cheddar cheese, divided
4 cups Chili Gravy (page 66, or any leftover chili)

Steps
1. Preheat your oven to 350°F.
2. Into the bottom of a medium baking dish, layer 2 cups of corn chips.
3. Layer on half of the onions and half of the cheese.
4. Spoon the Chili Gravy atop.
5. Layer on the remaining onions and cheese.
6. Place the remaining chips atop.
7. Place into the oven and bake 20 minutes.
8. Remove from the oven and let cool slightly before serving.

Chicken and Dumplings

(Serves 4)

Chicken and Dumplings is the ultimate American dish. No matter where you travel in America, you will find someplace that makes homemade Chicken and Dumplings. When it comes to Sunday dinner, there was a time when Chicken and Dumplings was almost mandatory. So, what is Chicken and Dumplings? In its original form, it is basically a chicken soup with little globs of dough.

When most eateries make Chicken and Dumplings, they do so with leftover chicken. There is nothing wrong with this, and I often do this too. In this case, you use a previously prepared chicken stock. When you make Chicken and Dumplings totally from scratch, you are making the chicken stock as you are cooking the chicken. Either way you go, you are in for a great, tasty treat, especially during the autumn and winter months.

This recipe will be in two parts: one for the chicken and then the other for the dumplings. Yes, the dumpling are made separate and then added to the chicken for a final round of cooking. You will notice I recommend NOT peeling the onion, and the reason is that the skin of the onion holds a lot of flavor and nutrients. If you have never had Chicken and Dumplings, you cannot truly say you've eaten American food. Do yourself a favor and make this one of your next family meals.

For the chicken soup

1 chicken, either whole or cut up
8 cups water
3 ribs celery, chopped
3 carrots, chopped
1 yellow onion, unpeeled and quartered
2 tsp. salt
4 cloves garlic, whole and unpeeled
2 bay leaves
1 tsp. black peppercorn

Steps

1. Place all of the ingredients into a large stock pot over high heat and bring to a boil.

2. Reduce the heat to a simmer and cook 90 minutes.

3. Remove the chicken from the pot and set aside to cool.

4. Strain the chicken stock into another pot or large bowl. Set the stock aside. Discard the solids.

5. Remove the chicken meat from the bones. Discard the bones and skin.

6. Set the chicken aside.

For the dumplings

2 cups flour
1 Tbs. baking powder
1 tsp. salt
2 eggs, beaten
⅔ cup milk
½ tsp. ground black pepper

Steps

1. In a medium bowl, whisk the flour, baking powder, and salt.

2. Stir in the eggs, milk, and black pepper to make a dough.

3. Let the dough rest 10 minutes.

4. Bring the chicken stock to a boil over high heat.

5. Drop tablespoon portions of the dough into the chicken stock.

6. Reduce the heat to a simmer, cover, and cook 15 minutes (the dumplings will grow).

7. Remove the stock and dumplings from the heat.

8. Stir the chicken into the stock.

9. Ladle the Chicken and Dumplings into serving bowls and enjoy.

Chicken Fried Steak

(Serves 4)

Well, hell, is it chicken or is it steak? This was my first question when I first ordered this dish when I was a teenager, and my family stopped at a diner on our way to Arkansas from San Francisco. My mother said it was a combination. Not a good thing to say to an inquisitive teen as my mind started to think, "How in the hell did they mate?!"

So, what is a Chicken Fried Steak, other than a classic American dish created somewhere in the South or Midwest? It is a piece of beef (usually the cut known as round steak), which is breaded like fried chicken and then fried. So there you have the very unimaginative name of Chicken Fried Steak.

The secret to a good Chicken Fried Steak is not so much the Chicken Fried Steak itself. The secret to a good one is the gravy. Yes, there is a special gravy for Chicken Fried Steak, and you will be able to find a recipe for it on page 218.

Ingredients

2 pounds round steak, each ½-inch thick
1 cup milk
¼ cup apple cider vinegar
1½ cups flour
½ cup yellow cornmeal
1 tsp. salt
½ tsp. ground black pepper
½ cup buttermilk
corn oil for frying
Chicken Fried Steak Gravy (page 218)

Steps

1. Place the steaks into a shallow bowl.
2. In a medium bowl, whisk the milk and vinegar.
3. Pour the milk mixture over the steaks and let them soak 20 minutes at room temperature (this will tenderize the steaks).
4. Remove the steaks and pat dry with paper towels.
5. In a shallow bowl, whisk the flour, cornmeal, salt, and pepper.
6. Pour the buttermilk into a shallow bowl.

7. Dredge (coat) the steaks in the seasoned flour.

8. Dip the dredged steaks in the buttermilk.

9. Re-dredge (coat) the steaks in the seasoned flour mixture.

10. Heat 1 inch of oil in a large sauté pan or skillet over medium heat.

11. Add the steaks and fry 8 minutes per side (time may vary depending on the thickness of the steaks).

12. Remove the steaks to a paper towel–lined plate.

13. Place the steaks on serving plates, drape with Chicken Fried Steak Gravy, and enjoy.

Chicken Pot Pie

(Serves 4)

The first introduction that most people have to Chicken Pot Pie is those little frozen things you buy in the store. They're good for a little snack, but they are in no way even close to a real Chicken Pot Pie. If you have never enjoyed a Chicken Pot Pie, I guess the best way to describe them would be that they are a chicken casserole embedded in a wonderful pastry crust. And how did this dish get its name, you ask? It is essentially a one-pot meal put inside a pie.

Whereas most home cooks make a Chicken Pot Pie by cooking a chicken and then removing the meat and following the recipe, diners and other such eateries used a different approach. They used leftover chicken. Matter of fact, the chicken chain KFC used to make their pot pies (very good, I might add) doing the same thing.

This recipe will be given in two parts. The first will be for the chicken, and the second will be for the pastry crust. To be authentic, you will want to use lard for your crust. I do not know why people fear lard as much as they do. It is really nothing more than rendered animal fat. You can, if you must, use a vegetable shortening instead of lard.

For the chicken

½ cup cream
2 cloves garlic, minced
3 Tbs. butter
½ onion, chopped
2 ribs celery, chopped
½ sweet red bell pepper, chopped
3 cups chicken stock
2 carrots, chopped
1 potato, diced
1 cup corn kernels
½ cup peas
1½ pounds cooked chicken meat, chopped
2 Tbs. flour
1 tsp. salt
½ tsp. ground black pepper

Steps

1. Preheat your oven to 400°F.

2. In a small pan over medium heat, stir the cream and garlic just until it comes to a simmer. Remove the pan from the heat.

3. In a large sauté pan or skillet, melt the butter over medium heat. Add the onion, celery, and red bell pepper and sauté 3 minutes.

4. Add the chicken stock and bring to a simmer.

5. Add the carrots and potato and cook 10 minutes.

6. Add the corn, peas, and chicken and cook 5 minutes.

7. In a small bowl, whisk the flour, salt, and pepper.

8. Stir the flour mixture into the pan and bring to a boil while stirring.

9. Reduce the heat to a simmer and cook 5 minutes to thicken.

10. Remove the pan from the heat, stir in the cream mixture, and fill the crust (see next section of recipe).

11. Place the top crust over the chicken mixture.

12. Place into the oven and bake 20 minutes.

13. Reduce the heat to 350°F and bake 30 minutes.

14. Remove from the oven and let cool slightly before serving.

(Continued on next page.)

For the pastry crust

¼ cup lard
¼ cup butter, chilled and diced
¼ cup shortening
2 cups flour
1 Tbs. salt
¼ cup ice water

Steps

1. In a large bowl, combine the lard, butter, shortening, flour, and salt. Using a pastry blender, cut them into the flour until the texture is crumbly.

2. Gradually stir in the ice water, a ½ tablespoon at a time, to form a dough.

3. Place the dough on a floured surface and knead a few minutes.

4. Divide the dough in half and wrap each half in plastic wrap and chill 30 minutes.

5. Place one half of the dough on a floured surface and roll out to fit a deep-dish 9-inch pie pan.

6. Place the dough in the pan and prick all over with a fork.

7. On a floured surface, roll out the other half of the dough to be the top crust for the Chicken Pot Pie.

··· **Note** ···

When making this pastry crust, adding the water at a slow pace is important as the humidity in your kitchen at any given time may affect the moisture of your dough. You may find that you don't need all of the ice water, or perhaps you need a little bit more than called for.

Creamed Chicken

(Serves 4)

I've always considered this dish to be a chicken pot pie without the pie. It is creamy goodness laden with chopped chicken and is the perfect meal to serve on one of those chilly autumn or winter days. It is also the epitome of the term "rib-sticking food."

This has always been a popular dish throughout the eateries of America, and it is usually served over homemade Buttermilk Biscuits (page 8) or Cream Biscuits (page 11). Once the gravy starts to soak through the biscuits, each forkful will literally melt in your mouth. This dish does call for Cream of Mushroom Soup; you can use the canned variety as long as it is low in sodium, or you can make your own with my recipe on page 70.

To be authentic, this dish is made with chicken breast meat. At many eateries, however, it is made with leftover chicken, which includes the dark meat (leg and thigh). I have made it both ways, and there really is not a difference other than the fact that you do not have to cook the chicken if you're using leftovers. By the way, you will notice the short cooking time for the chicken. Remember, chicken breasts cook faster than any other part of the chicken because it contains virtually no fat. If your chicken breasts are plumper than usual, just increase the cooking time.

Ingredients

2 Tbs. butter
1 yellow onion, chopped
4 cloves garlic, minced
¼ cup chicken stock

6 chicken breasts, boneless, skinless, and chopped
1 tsp. salt
½ tsp. ground paprika
10¾-ounce can Cream of Mushroom Soup (or homemade, see page 70)
½ cup sour cream

Steps

1. In a large saucepan, melt the butter over medium heat.
2. Add the onion and garlic and sauté 5 minutes.
3. Stir in the chicken stock, chicken, salt, and paprika and cook 10 minutes.
4. In a medium bowl, whisk the Cream of Mushroom Soup and the sour cream.
5. Stir the soup mixture into the pan and cook 10 minutes.
6. Ladle over biscuits and enjoy.

Cider Chops

(Serves 4)

A little unknown fact regarding apple cider vinegar since you will be seeing that ingredient a lot in this book: It is one of the best natural meat tenderizers you will ever find. When you are marinating meat in it (such as with this dish), you will want to remember not to marinate more than thirty minutes or the acid in the vinegar will begin to essentially cook the meat.

What type of pork chop should you use for Cider Chops? Good question, and I am glad you were thinking about it. Really, you could use any type from thin to thick and bone-in to boneless. You could also do what I do and cut your chops from a pork tenderloin. It really doesn't matter. I would, however, recommend removing any excess fat from the chop before you put them in the pan.

This dish, as do many which feature apple cider vinegar, originated in the South, and it was probably the type of dish one would call a "farm dish." Farm dishes were always rather quick to make and consisted of foods that go well with biscuits or cornbread—and Cider Chops are wonderful with either one of them.

Ingredients

1 cup water
1 cup apple cider vinegar
1 yellow onion, chopped
5 cloves garlic, minced
¼ tsp. ground cumin
4 pork chops, trimmed of excess fat
¼ cup flour
3 Tbs. corn oil

Steps

1. In a medium shallow bowl, whisk the water, vinegar, onion, garlic, and cumin.
2. Add the pork chops and turn a few times to coat them.
3. Marinate the pork chops 30 minutes at room temperature.
4. Place the flour in a shallow bowl.
5. In a medium sauté pan or skillet, heat the oil over medium heat.
6. Remove the pork chops from the marinade and dredge (coat) them in the flour.

7. Place the pork chops in the pan and fry 8–10 minutes per side (depending on thickness).

8. Place the pork chops on a serving platter and enjoy.

Cider Pot Roast

(Serves 4)

Pot roast. It may actually be the most authentic one-pot meal in the culinary arts. You have meat, you have vegetables, and you have gravy. What more can you ask for . . . besides a glass of a good Napa Valley wine to drink with it. The pot roast is classic American fare, and it doesn't matter which coast you are on—if you go into any diner or roadside eatery, at least once a week, a pot roast is going to be the famed Blue Plate Special.

And I'll tell you another great thing about pot roast. You can use any cut of beef your little heart (or littler bank account) desires. Because of the way a pot roast is cooked (a long time in liquid), it will tenderize the toughest cut of beef, and in the case of this version, Cider Pot Roast, it is even truer because of the use of apple cider, a natural meat tenderizer.

When it comes to a pot roast, here is something that has always bugged me (same for stew too). Why do people cut their vegetables so small? Stop it! Due to the cooking process, the vegetables should not be diced into little pieces. They turn into mush. Cut the veggies rather large, and you will not only get more flavor, but their texture will be wonderful as well.

Ingredients

1 Tbs. corn oil
4-pound chuck roast, trimmed of excess fat
2 cups apple cider
2 white onions, chopped
4 ribs celery, chopped
½ tsp. ground allspice
½ tsp. ground ginger
2 bay leaves
1 tsp. ground black pepper
6 whole cloves
8 red potatoes, peeled and quartered
6 carrots, chopped
2 Tbs. butter, softened
2 Tbs. flour

Steps

1. Preheat your oven to 300°F (yes, that low).
2. In a large oven-proof sauté pan, heat the oil over medium heat.
3. Add the chuck roast and brown on all sides.
4. Into the pan, add the apple cider, onions, celery, allspice, ginger, bay leaves, pepper, and cloves. Stir all the ingredients to blend.
5. Place a lid on the pan, place into the oven, and cook 2½ hours, turning the meat twice.
6. Add the potatoes and carrots, place the cover on the pan, and cook 90 additional minutes.
7. Remove the meat and vegetables to a serving platter.
8. Place the pan back on the burner over medium heat and remove the bay leaves and whole cloves.
9. In a small bowl, whisk the butter and flour to form a paste.
10. Whisk the paste into the gravy and cook until thickened.
11. Spoon the gravy over the meat and vegetables and enjoy.

Cola Chicken

(Serves 4)

Well, a lot of people drink cola while eating fried chicken, so maybe it makes sense to simply douse the chicken in cola before frying it. Something tells me this dish probably originated somewhere near Atlanta, Georgia, where the headquarters of a famous cola maker are located. When I first saw this dish on a menu in the South I said to myself, "If you don't order this, you'll kick yourself for the rest of your life." So I ordered it. It was good!

You don't really cook the chicken in the cola. You soak the chicken in the cola, and this does make a lot of sense. The carbonation from the soda can actually make meat more tender, and in the case of chicken, the carbonation can get under the skin with the little bubbles. If you decide to make this dish, be advised there is a twenty-four hour soaking period.

So now let's answer the age-old question of whether it is cheaper to buy chicken cut-up or to cut it yourself. Let's assume neither whole nor cut-up chicken is on sale; it will be cheaper to cut it up into serving pieces yourself, plus you get the bonus of saving the excess parts (skin, fat, bones) for your stock pot.

Ingredients

1 chicken, cut into serving pieces
2 cups cola
1½ Tbs. salt
1 Tbs. ground black pepper
1 Tbs. Worcestershire sauce
1 Tbs. hot sauce
corn oil for frying
2 cups flour
1 tsp. garlic salt
1 tsp. ground paprika

Steps

1. Place the chicken in a large shallow bowl.
2. In a large bowl, stir the cola, salt, pepper, Worcestershire sauce, and hot sauce.
3. Pour the cola mixture over the chicken. Cover the bowl and let marinate overnight in the refrigerator.

4. Heat 2 inches of corn oil in a large sauté pan or skillet until it reaches 325°F on a deep-fry thermometer.

5. Drain the chicken and pat dry.

6. In a ziplock bag, combine the flour, garlic salt, and paprika.

7. Place the chicken in the bag and dredge (coat) the chicken with the seasoned flour.

8. Carefully place the chicken in the hot oil and fry about 15 minutes per side.

9. Remove the chicken to a paper towel–lined plate.

10. Place the chicken on a serving platter and enjoy.

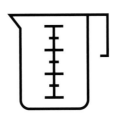

Corn-Fried Shrimp

(Serves 4)

One of the more popular dishes served at diners and roadside eateries is a basket of fried shrimp. There is nothing quite like that red plastic basket lined with paper coming to your table or booth with a heaping collection of yumminess and that always too-small bowl of tartar sauce. If you have ever enjoyed this true piece of Americana, you have noticed the special crunch to these shrimp. That crunch is created by the simple inclusion of cornmeal in the batter.

Corn-Fried Shrimp is indeed a comfort food for many people (including myself). When it is made from scratch, even the aroma is comforting. For the best results when preparing this dish, you want to use a medium-sized shrimp. The most popular of this size is called a tiger shrimp. To be truly authentic when making Corn-Fried Shrimp, you will want to leave the tail section with the shell on it.

Deep frying is an art form, and in order to master this art form, you must have a deep-fry thermometer. They are quite inexpensive and can be purchased at any kitchenware store. Even if you have an electric deep fryer, have a deep-fry thermometer handy because I have never seen a deep fryer with a temperature control that works properly.

Ingredients
1 pound medium shrimp, shelled except for the tail portion
¾ cup yellow cornmeal
¾ cup flour
2 tsp. ground black pepper
1 Tbs. ground paprika
¾ cup buttermilk
2 tsp. onion powder
2 tsp. garlic salt
1 tsp. hot sauce
corn oil for frying

Steps
1. Rinse the shrimp under cold water and pat dry.
2. In a large bowl, whisk the cornmeal, flour, black pepper, and paprika.
3. In a medium bowl, whisk the buttermilk, onion powder, garlic salt, and hot sauce.

4. In a large skillet heat 4 inches of oil to 350°F on a deep-fry thermometer.
5. Dredge (coat) the shrimp in the flour mixture.
6. Dip the dredged shrimp into the buttermilk mixture.
7. Once again dredge the shrimp in the flour mixture.
8. Carefully place the shrimp into the hot oil and deep fry until golden.
9. Remove the shrimp to a paper towel–lined plate.
10. Let the Corn-Fried Shrimp cool slightly before serving.

Country Baked Cider Ribs

(Serves 4)

Ribs! Everyone loves ribs. There is just something about gnawing on a bone which brings out the primitive in all humans. It's like when we eat a banana, and our primate instincts become rather evident. Whereas ribs are most often grilled or broiled, this is usually difficult to do in an eatery, so the way they prepared ribs is by baking them. Baked ribs are quite good and oftentimes much more tender than their grilled or broiled counterparts.

In most eateries which feature ribs, the ribs of choice are usually what are referred to as St. Louis ribs. They have a little more meat on them and are usually less expensive. They are also generally a little less tender than baby back ribs or prime rib bones, but no need to worry because this recipe will make them tender due to both the cooking process and the use of apple cider, a natural meat tenderizer.

This particular rib dish is very Southern in nature. It has a wonderful sauce featuring apple cider and molasses, and as is the case with most dishes of this ilk, it is very simple to prepare. Once the ribs are cooked, you will then thicken the sauce the old-fashioned way—with heat!

Ingredients

1 Tbs. corn oil
4 pounds St. Louis–style ribs
1 Tbs. flour
1½ cups apple cider
1½ cups water
1 Tbs. molasses
1 tsp. dried rosemary, crumbled
1 tsp. salt
½ tsp. ground black pepper

Steps

1. In a large skillet or sauté pan, heat the oil over medium heat.
2. Add the ribs and brown on both sides.
3. Remove the ribs from the pan and set aside.
4. Reduce the heat to low under the pan and whisk in the four and apple cider until thick.
5. Stir in the water, molasses, rosemary, salt, and pepper until smooth.

6. Place the ribs back into the pan (in layers if necessary).
7. Place into the oven and bake 1 hour.
8. Remove the ribs from the pan and place on a serving platter.
9. Place the pan over high heat and stir the sauce until it has thickened.
10. Drape the sauce over the ribs and enjoy!

Cream Chipped Beef

(Serves 4)

There are people who absolutely love this dish. There are people who crave this dish. There are people who have fought over this dish. And then there are people who refer to it by its nickname, which is "shit on a shingle"—and I really have no idea what that means, but it is also what my mother called it.

Being an inquisitive child, I ordered this dish during a family outing to Reno at the Nugget Casino. My mother warned me about it. I didn't listen (typical teen). It was served over points of toast (a fancy term meaning toast cut into quarters). It was interesting, and I can't really say that it was bad. Regardless, it is indeed an American tradition.

So what is chipped beef? It is a dried beef which is thinly sliced. Back in the day, I will assume it was a very dried beef, and they literally chipped pieces off of it. This dish does go back quite far and was often cooked on the wagon trains. Nowadays, you can usually find chipped beef in jars in the area where canned and processed meats are located in your supermarket. It is an interesting dish. Try it!

Ingredients

2 Tbs. bacon fat
2 Tbs. flour
2 cups milk
2½ ounces chipped beef
½ tsp. ground black pepper

Steps

1. In a medium skillet, heat the bacon fat over medium heat.

2. Whisk in the flour until smooth.

3. Slowly whisk in the milk until thick and creamy.

4. Stir in the chipped beef and black pepper. Lower the heat to low and cook 3 minutes (just long enough to heat the meat).

5. Serve over toast and enjoy.

Fried Catfish

(Serves 4)

. . . And then there is catfish. If you have ever been to the South, you have eaten catfish. You might not have known it, but you have. If you have ever seen a movie set in the South, you have heard of catfish, and chances are, there was more than one dinner prepared with it. Catfish is a staple of Southern cooking, and whether you like it or not simply depends on the way it is prepared.

So, what is a catfish? No, there is no relation to a feline here. It gets its name due to its facial barbels (facial feelers) which resemble a cat's whiskers. They are a rather ugly fish, sometimes very bony (depending on the species), and they have teeth! I prefer others catch them for me to cook.

Catfish are a very popular food staple throughout the world, and where you are determines how they are cooked. In the Southern regions of America, the most popular way to cook these ugly little creatures of the water is quite simple: a very coarse cornmeal batter and then plopped in some hot oil. You can buy catfish at most markets with a decent seafood area.

Ingredients

2 cups yellow mustard
2 cups yellow cornmeal
2 pounds filleted catfish
corn oil for frying

Steps

1. Spread the mustard over the catfish.
2. Coat the catfish with the cornmeal and set aside.
3. In a large sauté pan or skillet, heat a few inches of oil to 325°F on a deep-fry thermometer.
4. Carefully place the catfish into the oil and fry 5 minutes per side.
5. Remove the catfish to a paper towel–lined plate to remove any excess oil.
6. Let the catfish cool slightly before serving.
7. Remove from the oven and let cool slightly before serving.

Dirty Fried Chicken

(Serves 4)

Don't you just love some of the names people give to dishes? Dirty Fried Chicken. Doesn't really have the most appetizing moniker. This one of the many ways Southerners prepare fried chicken, and like all of their ways, it is quite good, despite the rather soiled name.

Why is this dish called Dirty Fried Chicken? I have no idea. When I first started to play with this recipe, I thought maybe because it had a lot of ground black pepper in it, and pepper is black so it would look like dirt. Well, once cooked, it doesn't really look dirty (which is indeed a good thing). So, I gave up trying to figure out why someone would name it as such, and instead, I just ate it.

One thing about this chicken which I find quite appealing (and delicious) is the fact that the seasoned mixture you dredge (coat) the chicken in is quite different than any other. Also, while it is being fried, it sends quite a nice aroma wafting through the kitchen. Dirty Fried Chicken is a wonderful addition to your fried chicken recipe collection.

Ingredients
corn oil for frying
1 tsp. ground paprika
1 tsp. dried mustard
1 tsp. onion powder
1 tsp. ground black pepper
1 tsp. dried sage, crumbled
1 cup flour
1 chicken, cut into serving pieces

Steps
1. In a large sauté pan or skillet, heat 3 inches of corn oil to 325°F on a deep-fry thermometer.
2. In a ziplock bag, combine the paprika, mustard, onion powder, black pepper, sage, and flour.
3. Place the chicken in the bag and shake to dredge (coat).
4. Carefully place the chicken in the pan, skin-side down, and fry 5 minutes per side.
5. Lower the heat, place a lid on the pan, and fry for 7 minutes per side.

6. Remove the chicken to a paper towel–lined plate.
7. Let the chicken cool slightly before serving.

Homesteader Fried Chicken

(Serves 4)

To be totally blunt, fried chicken is simply a way of life in America. From my way of thinking, a home without fried chicken is not a home. It is one of the few foods that is equally delicious hot or cold. If there are any leftovers, it is the most versatile dish on the planet. If fried chicken is not cooked at least once a week in my humble abode, call the coroner because I have died!

Homesteader Fried Chicken is the easiest and simplest fried chicken on the planet. If you can turn on the heat and know how to tell time, you cannot mess this dish up. There is one very important rule to this fried chicken, however, which must be strictly adhered to. You must only use buttermilk—real buttermilk—and none of that faux stuff.

The homesteaders would always fry their chicken in lard. You can too, but lard does get a little pricey. When I am making any American-style of fried chicken, I always use a corn oil because . . . well, because my mother did!

Ingredients
1 chicken, cut into serving pieces
½ cup buttermilk
1½ cups flour
1 tsp. ground black pepper
2 tsp. salt
lard or corn oil, for frying

Steps
1. Place the chicken into a shallow bowl.
2. Pour the buttermilk over the chicken and turn it a few times to coat.
3. Place a piece of plastic wrap over the chicken and chill two hours, turning once.
4. In a ziplock bag, combine the flour, pepper, and salt.
5. In a large sauté pan or skillet, heat 1 inch of oil to 325°F on a deep-fry thermometer.
6. Remove the chicken from the buttermilk.
7. Place the chicken in the bag of flour and dredge (coat).

8. Carefully place the chicken into the oil and fry 5 minutes per side.
9. Reduce the heat to low, cover, and fry 10 minutes per side.
10. Remove the chicken to a paper towel–lined plate.
11. Let the chicken cool slightly before serving.

Milk Fried Chicken

(Serves 4)

No, this chicken is not fried in milk. Nothing on Earth is ever fried in milk. I don't know why frying is associated with milk in this title. Perhaps the title would be a little more appropriate if it was called Fried Milk Chicken. I don't know. I do know it is interesting and fun to make, and it is pretty damn good!

Let's face a fact, if it can be fried, it can be found in the South. My lord, these people love their fried foods. Lucky for us, one of the foods they love to fry is chicken, and they are always willing to share. When I first saw this fried chicken on a diner menu in the South, I immediately knew I had to order it. What is there not to love here? You have chicken and milk . . . well, sort of.

The milk for this dish is actually evaporated milk. The milk is used for soaking the chicken. Once the chicken is fried, it gives it a distinctive flavor. I also like the coating here. It is a blend of flour and cornmeal and has a nice subtle Southern crunch. This is a very good addition to your collection of fried chicken recipes.

Ingredients

12-ounce can evaporated milk
1 Tbs. Worcestershire sauce
1 tsp. ground cayenne
1 chicken, cut into serving pieces
corn oil for frying
¾ cup flour
¾ cup yellow cornmeal
1 tsp. salt
½ tsp. ground black pepper

Steps

1. In a large bowl, whisk the evaporated milk, Worcestershire sauce, and cayenne.
2. Add the chicken, cover, and chill overnight.
3. In a large sauté pan or skillet, heat 2 inches of oil to 325°F on a deep-fry thermometer.
4. In a ziplock bag, combine the flour, cornmeal, salt, and pepper.
5. Remove the chicken from the milk.

6. Place the chicken into the ziplock bag and dredge (coat) with the seasoned flour.
7. Carefully place the chicken into the oil and fry 5 minutes per side.
8. Lower the heat to low, cover, and fry 10 minutes per side.
9. Remove the chicken to a paper towel–lined plate.
10. Let the chicken cool slightly before serving.

Old Fashioned Lamb Pie

(Serves 4)

The origins of lamb pie go back before the days of Christ. It was a dish, according to lore, created by Middle Eastern shepherds—which makes sense because who would have more fresh lamb than a shepherd? If you have never enjoyed a lamb pie, just think of it as a pot pie made with lamb because, well, that really is what it is.

I love lamb pie, and when I make it, I always use whatever portions of lamb meat is cheapest at the market. Why? Because of the cooking process, even the cheapest cuts of lamb will be tender. No need to spend a lot of money. What you do want to be careful of is the amount of fat on the lamb. Remember, you're paying per pound, and fat isn't light. Go for less fat, and you'll be fine.

As far as the pie crust for this Old Fashioned Lamb Pie, you can go two ways. You can make your own and use the pie crust recipe I have included on page 276, or you can use a good quality frozen pie crust.

Ingredients

2 Tbs. olive oil
1 yellow onion, chopped
2 pounds lamb meat, trimmed of excess fat and roughly chopped or cubed
2 cups beef stock
1 cup dry white wine
1 tsp. curry powder
¼ tsp. ground cloves
1 bay leaf
4 small red potatoes, peeled and diced
4 carrots, peeled and diced
¼ cup cornstarch
one 9-inch pie crust (page 276)

Steps

1. In a large sauté pan or skillet, heat the oil over medium heat.
2. Add the onion and sauté 5 minutes.
3. Add the lamb meat and cook 10 minutes.
4. Stir in the stock, wine, curry powder, cloves, and bay leaf and bring to a boil.

5. Lower the heat to a simmer and cook 20 minutes.

6. Preheat your oven to 350°F.

7. Remove and discard the bay leaf. Add the potatoes and carrots.

8. Stir in the cornstarch and bring to a boil (the sauce will thicken).

9. Remove the pan from the heat.

10. Spoon the mixture into the pie shell and loosely cover with foil.

11. Place into the oven and bake 30 minutes.

12. Remove from the oven and let cool slightly before cutting and serving.

··· **Note** ···

There is no top crust for the lamb pie.
You only need the bottom crust!

Penn State Pot Roast

(Serves 4)

Depending on who you are, where you were raised, and the food you like, I think it is a pretty good bet that most of the dishes we're presenting in this Blue Plate Special section will conjure up memories and are also a few of your go-to comfort foods. One of the most popular comfort foods in America is pot roast. We all grew up with the aroma of a pot roast wafting through the house. Even as I write about it, I am salivating.

I first had this adaptation of pot roast at a roadside eatery in the beautiful state of Pennsylvania. The meat almost literally melted in my mouth. I like this version a lot because, as opposed to most other pot roasts I have had, it was only meat. There were no vegetables. To me, a pot roast with a lot of vegetables is basically a stew! This was served over some luscious, creamy mashed potatoes, and it was indeed a memorable meal.

The cut of beef to use for this pot roast (or most pot roasts for that matter) is the brisket. The long course of heating is perfect for this cut of meat, and it will tenderize it perfectly. Since the brisket can often have a lot of fat on it, make sure to trim before you start cooking it. By the way, if you don't know what a beef brisket is, you might know it from the name it has when it is salt-cured, and that is a corned beef.

Ingredients

1 Tbs. olive oil
3-pound beef brisket, trimmed
8 cloves garlic, minced
1½ tsp. dried thyme, crumbled
1 tsp. salt
1 tsp. ground black pepper
2 yellow onions, chopped
1 sweet red onion, thinly sliced
1 cup beef stock
2 Tbs. tomato paste
2 cups dry red wine

Steps

1. Preheat your oven to 300°F (yes, that low).
2. In a large sauté pan or skillet, heat the oil over medium-high heat.

3. Place the brisket in the pan and brown on both sides.

4. In a small bowl, combine the garlic, thyme, salt, and pepper. Rub the mixture over the brisket.

5. Place the yellow and red onions over the meat.

6. Place the pan into the oven and roast 60 minutes.

7. In a medium bowl, whisk the beef stock, tomato paste, and red wine.

8. Pour liquid over the meat and roast 3½ hours.

9. Remove pan from the oven.

10. Place the meat on a serving platter and thinly slice.

11. Spoon the sauce over the meat and serve.

Pepper Steak

(Serves 4)

I am sure the origins of Pepper Steak is in France, but the popularity of Pepper Steak is definitely American. If you go into any chop house or steak house, you will find Pepper Steak. You might even find a version of Pepper Steak at some diners, minus the brandy of course. By the way, the "pepper" in Pepper Steak has nothing to do with the fruit pepper (yes, peppers are a fruit), but with the spice known as pepper—as in black pepper.

The most important element in making a perfect Pepper Steak is the cut of meat. You want a very good quality steak, and it must be marbled (meaning there is fat running through the flesh). This will guarantee that your Pepper Steak will be flavorful and tender. The next rule is in the cooking (grilling or pan-frying) the Pepper Steak. For the utmost in taste and texture, it should never be done above medium-rare. Once past that point, the flavor of the meat diminishes very rapidly. Yes, you want blood on the plate!

This dish does contain alcohol. It has a hefty addition of brandy. No, alcohol does not fully burn off once it has been cooked. There is no substitution here. It cannot be an actual Pepper Steak without this. Sorry, this is just one of the rules of the game.

Ingredients

4 well-marbled steaks, preferably rather thick
½ cup crushed black peppercorns (or a very coarse ground)
¼ cup butter, divided
2 shallots, minced
½ sweet yellow onion, minced
½ cup brandy (or good-quality bourbon)

Steps

1. Heat a grill or grill pan over medium-high heat.
2. Place the steaks on a hard surface and sprinkle with the pepper.
3. Using a flat, heavy object, pound the pepper into the steaks.
4. Place the steaks on the grill or grill pan and spread the tops with half of the butter.
5. In a small pan over medium heat, add the remaining 2 tablespoons of butter, shallots, and onion and sauté 2 minutes.
6. Remove the pan from the heat and stir in the brandy.
7. Place the pan back on the heat and bring to a boil.

8. On the grill (or grill pan), turn the steaks over and grill a few minutes.

9. Place the steaks on serving plates.

10. Spoon some sauce over the steaks and serve.

Plugged Port Pork Roast

(Serves 4)

There are a couple of very chic diners throughout California's wine country that feature pork roast on their menu. They do some marvelous things with these roasts, which are often presented as a meal for two. One of my favorites was this Plugged Port Pork Roast which is an adaptation of one of my original dishes.

For this dish, the best method is to cut your own roast from a pork tenderloin. It will be much more flavorful, and you won't have to put up with the usual amounts of fat. In most cases, depending on your market, it will also be cheaper. For safety's and health's sake, always remember to cook your pork roast to 150–160°F on a meat thermometer.

Plugging a pork roast (or leg of lamb) is a very simple process. The only tool you will need is a sharp paring knife (small knife). What you do is cut a deep gash into the meat. Into that gash, you place a whole, peeled clove of garlic. That is it. You do want to make sure the gash is deep enough to fit the whole clove, or they will fall out during the roasting process because meat shrinks when it is cooked.

Ingredients

5 cloves garlic, peeled
1 tsp. salt
2 Tbs. minced fresh rosemary
2 Tbs. olive oil
1 tsp. ground black pepper
2-pound pork roast
2 scallions (green onions), chopped
½ cup port wine
½ cup water

Steps

1. Preheat your oven to 350°F.
2. Plug the pork roast with the garlic (see note above).
3. In a small bowl, combine the salt, rosemary, olive oil, and black pepper.
4. Rub the mixture all over the pork roast.
5. In a medium roasting pan, place the scallions, then pour in the port and water.
6. Place the pork roast into the roasting pan.

7. Place into the oven and roast 45 minutes or until 150–160°F on a meat thermometer.

8. Remove the pork roast to a carving board and let rest 5 minutes.

9. Slice the pork roast thinly and place on a serving platter.

10. Spoon the sauce over the meat and serve.

Pot Roast with Gingersnap Gravy

(Serves 4)

As opposed to our other pot roast dishes in this chapter, this one may be a little more along the lines of what you are used to. It is a pot roast resembling a stew, but this one has a little twist as you might have noticed from the title. With this pot roast, the gravy is influenced by gingersnaps. Yes, the cookie!

From what I have been able to determine, Gingersnap Gravy was either conceived in Northern Europe or in the New England region of America. My guess is, it may have originated in Europe and was then brought over to this country. Regardless of its origin, it is quite tasty, and the slight sweetness is pure perfection.

The best cut of beef for this pot roast is a cut known as a chuck roast. It is not the best quality cut of beef, but due to the cooking process here, you don't need a great cut. Because of the long cooking process in liquid, this "cheap" cut of beef will be wonderfully tender by the time it hits your plate.

Ingredients

¼ cup corn oil

4-pound chuck roast, trimmed of excess fat

2 yellow onions, chopped

4 cloves garlic, minced

2 Tbs. flour

4 cups beef stock

4 carrots, chopped

4 ribs celery, chopped

2 Tbs. brown sugar

12 gingersnap cookies, crumbled

Steps

1. Preheat your oven to 325°F.

2. In a large sauté pan or skillet, heat the oil over medium heat.

3. Add the beef and brown on top and bottom.

4. Remove the meat to a platter and set aside.

5. Into the pan, add the onions and garlic and sauté 5 minutes.

6. Stir in the flour and stock; add the carrots, celery, brown sugar, and cookies. Bring the mixture to a simmer.

7. Place the meat back into the pan, cover, and braise in the oven 3 hours (turning the meat about four times during this period).

8. Remove the meat to a carving board and let rest 5 minutes.

9. Skim off any fat from the gravy.

10. Thinly slice the meat and place on a serving platter.

11. Spoon the vegetables around the meat.

12. Spoon the gravy over the meat and serve.

··· **Note** ···

Why the low oven temperature and long cooking time? The braising process and length will tenderize the chuck roast, which is usually a tough cut.

Roast Beef Hash

(Serves 4)

Did you know that, most of the time when you order corned beef hash at an eatery, you are actually getting a roast beef hash? It's true! Doesn't really matter though since you are still getting beef. Also of note is that, if you look at many menus, it will simply say "hash," and your mind has been trained to see "corned beef hash." The next logical question may be, "So is it corned beef in those cans?" I don't know, but I do know it doesn't look like any corned beef I have ever had.

There was a time in this great country we call America when the most popular use for leftover roast beef (or prime rib) was making hash—yes, even more often than the always yummy roast beef sandwiches. The reason this type of hash was so popular was because hash was not just a breakfast item; it was also a very popular dinner item. If you have never had real hash, I think you will be in for a big tasty surprise.

In the steps for this recipe, you will see that I call for you to mince the leftover roast beef. This is really quite important for even cooking of the entire dish. Remember, a "mince" is smaller than a "dice." You want to be able to pick up a little of everything with each forkfull of goodness. You cannot really make it too small, but you can make it too big.

Ingredients
2 Tbs. corn oil
1 Tbs. butter
2½ cups diced red potatoes
1 yellow onion, minced
1 sweet red bell pepper, minced
4 cups leftover minced roast beef
¾ cup beef stock
1 Tbs. ketchup
1 tsp. ground black pepper
1 tsp. salt

Steps
1. In a large sauté pan or skillet, melt the butter with the oil over medium heat.
2. Add the potatoes, onion, and bell pepper and sauté 10 minutes.
3. Stir in all the remaining ingredients and bring the mixture to a simmer.

4. Place a lid on the pan and cook 10 minutes.

5. Remove the cover from the pan and stir a few times to blend everything.

6. Keep cooking until all the liquid has evaporated and the bottom begins to crisp up.

7. Remove the pan from the heat.

8. Spoon the Roast Beef Hash onto a serving platter and enjoy.

Roasted Lemon Chicken

(Serves 4)

Is there really anything more comforting than Sunday dinner with a beautifully roasted chicken as the centerpiece of the table? It sounds like a script out of an old Henry Fonda movie, but the fact of the matter is this used to be a Sunday tradition for many families, including mine. Of course, back then the chicken contained more meat than chemicals, but I digress.

So, what is the best type of chicken to roast? There is a type of chicken called a "roaster"; it is bred for roasting. Then there is a "capon," which is a neutered rooster, and is pretty good-sized. Of course, you have the most popular, which is a "fryer." The chicken I often turn to for everything is the good old-fashioned fryer chicken. It is the perfect size for a family of four and has less fat.

This classic American way of preparing a chicken is quite interesting. It is simply a roasted chicken that is stuffed with a few lemons. What happens is that, during the roasting process, the essential oils from the lemon envelop the chicken, and this is why the chicken gets turned halfway through the roasting process. Of course, the citric acid from the lemons also naturally tenderize the chicken. Quite a good dish to invoke some Sunday dinner memories.

Ingredients

1 whole chicken
2 Tbs. olive oil
salt and pepper to taste
½ tsp. ground paprika
2 whole lemons

Steps

1. Preheat your oven to 350°F.
2. Rub the chicken all over with the olive oil.
3. Season the chicken with the salt, pepper, and paprika.
4. Place a roasting rack in a small roasting pan.
5. Place the chicken, breast side down, on the rack.
6. Pierce the lemons all over with the tines of a fork.
7. Place both lemons into the cavity of the chicken.
8. Place the chicken into the oven and roast 30 minutes.

9. Turn the chicken over and roast an additional 30 minutes.

10. Increase the heat to 400°F.

11. Turn the chicken over again and roast 15 minutes more.

12. Remove the chicken from the oven and place on a carving board.

13. Remove the lemons from the chicken and discard. Let the chicken rest 10 minutes.

14. Carve the chicken into serving pieces and serve.

Sloppy Joes

(Serves 4)

Is there really a more all-American Blue Plate Special more famous than the Sloppy Joe? I think not! Who would have ever thought that a toasted hamburger bun slopped with some gravy would become a legend. Sometimes it is the simplest dishes which mean the most. Give me a Sloppy Joe and a vanilla malt, and I will smile until the cows come home (I really have no idea what that adage means).

Sloppy Joes have been an American staple since the early 1940s and are considered one of the quintessential fast food originals. Aside from being known as Sloppy Joes, they are also known as Toasted Deviled Hamburgers, Chopped Meat Sandwiches, and Hamburger a la Creole. No matter what you might want to call it, if it is to be a true Sloppy Joe, it must have ground beef (hamburger) and none of this ground turkey or other such atrocities.

The burning question when it comes to Sloppy Joes is: Do you toast the bun or not? Hmmm. My mother never toasted the bun. Most diners will toast the bun. I think my preference is a toasted bun for absolutely no reason I can think of—I just like it. It really doesn't make a difference since the bun is going to get soggy anyway!

Ingredients

1½ pounds ground beef
1 yellow onion, chopped
1 sweet red bell pepper, chopped
8-ounce can tomato sauce
¾ cup ketchup
1 Tbs. Worcestershire sauce
1 tsp. yellow mustard
¼ cup sugar
1 tsp. garlic salt
Hamburger Buns (toasted or not) (page 26)

Steps

1. Heat a large sauté pan or skillet over medium heat.
2. Add the ground beef, onion, and bell pepper and cook 10 minutes or until the ground beef is browned.
3. Spoon out any rendered fat.

4. Stir in the tomato sauce, ketchup, Worcestershire, mustard, sugar, and garlic salt and bring to a boil.
5. Reduce the heat to a simmer and cook 20 minutes (giving it a few stirs during this time).
6. Place the buns on serving plates.
7. Spoon the Sloppy Joe mixture over the buns and enjoy!

Smothered Chicken

(Serves 4)

There is an adage in Southern cooking: "When in doubt, smother it!" Honestly, I kind of like this adage; it is not only used just in the South but in many areas of America where they like their food to be of the good old-fashioned, rib-sticking variety. There is nothing wrong with this, especially in the colder months of the year.

Smothered Chicken is a very tasty chicken casserole. It is also very high in fat, but as Julia Child was fond of saying, "You can eat anything as long as it is in moderation." With this dish, you are going to do something not too often done anymore but which was at one time a popular thing—you will be teaming chicken with bacon. Bacon! Yep, that got your attention.

There are two authentic ways to prepare Smothered Chicken, depending on which part of the country you're from. Away from the South, people will usually cut the chicken into serving pieces before cooking it. In the South, they leave the chicken whole. I prefer the Southern way and then cut the chicken into serving pieces once it is at the table.

Ingredients

1 whole chicken
12 slices bacon, cut in half
2 lemons, sliced
½ cup water
2 carrots, chopped
1 sweet yellow onion, thinly sliced
1 tsp. dried thyme, crumbled
2 tsp. salt
1 tsp. ground black pepper
1 tsp. sugar
½ tsp. ground allspice
½ cup chicken stock

Steps

1. Wash and dry the chicken and remember to take out the innards. (You can save the innards for making stock at a later time.)

2. In a pan/pot deep enough to eventually hold the chicken, over low heat, layer half of the bacon on the bottom.

3. Place the slices of lemon over the bacon and then top the lemon with the remaining bacon.

4. Pour the water over the bacon and cook 7 minutes.

5. Add the carrots, onions, thyme, salt, pepper, sugar, and allspice and cook 2 minutes.

6. Place the chicken into the pan and pour the stock over everything.

7. Bring to a boil. Reduce the heat to a simmer, cover, and cook 1 hour (basting a few times).

8. Remove the chicken to a serving platter and cut into serving pieces.

9. Spoon the bacon and vegetables around the chicken.

10. Spoon the sauce over all and enjoy.

Smothered Steak

(Serves 4)

Since we have gone from Smothered Chicken (page 202) to this Smothered Steak, you might think the only thing different is the meat. Well . . . you're wrong—kind of. Yes, the meat is different but, then again, so is the whole dish!

The idea of Smothered Steak (there are tons of adaptations for this dish) undoubtedly came about from some cook at a diner who decided the refrigerator was too full and, if he plopped a bunch of stuff on a cut of beef, it would sell. The idea has apparently worked since this is still quite a popular dish in diners and other such eateries around America. This particular adaptation of Smothered Steak is more along the lines of what you would find at a café in California or the great Northwest.

When making this version of Smothered Steak, I think the best piece of beef to use is what is referred to as a "London broil." You usually wouldn't cook a London broil in this way. It is usually grilled or broiled (thus the name), but due to the fact that it is pretty much a fat-free piece of beef, it handles the long cooking process quite well and will be very tender.

Ingredients

2-pound London broil, trimmed of any excess fat
¼ cup flour
1 Tbs. corn oil
2 sweet yellow onions, thinly sliced
1 cup beef stock
2 tomatoes, chopped
1 bay leaf
1 Tbs. freshly minced parsley
1 Tbs. Worcestershire sauce
1 Tbs. lemon juice
¼ tsp. ground cayenne pepper
1 tsp. salt
½ tsp. red pepper flakes

Steps

1. Dredge (coat) the London broil in flour.
2. In a large sauté pan or skillet, heat the oil over medium-high heat.

3. Place the London broil in the pan and cook 5 minutes per side.
4. Remove the London broil to a platter and set aside.
5. Into the pan, place the onions and sauté 5 minutes.
6. Stir in the stock and all remaining ingredients and bring to a boil.
7. Place the London broil back into the pan.
8. Reduce the heat to a simmer, cover, and cook 60 minutes.
9. Remove the London broil to a serving platter and thinly slice.
10. Spoon the juices and onions over the meat and serve.

Sweet Pickle Meatloaf

(Serves 4)

Meatloaf is as much a part of the American food landscape as apple pie. By that, I mean they both come from France! Seriously, they do, but both are considered true American foods—and both are the staple of a good diner or roadside eatery. Matter of fact, in the days of yore, if you ordered a meatloaf Blue Plate Special, the dessert included was always apple pie.

Elsewhere in this chapter, we have gone into some trivia regarding meatloaf (or meat loaf—both spellings are correct), so for this one, we will just venture into the world of flavor. When I first saw this meatloaf on a diner menu, it piqued my curiosity because of the inclusion of "sweet pickles." I love sweet pickles. I was not displeased to find they meant sweet-pickle relish because, well . . . that is essentially minced sweet pickles. I really like the flavor the sweet pickles give this meatloaf and found it to be quite enjoyable.

One thing you might notice about this meatloaf is the fact that there are no tomatoes associated with it. No tomato sauce. No ketchup. This is actually how original meatloaf was prepared. This makes for a wonderful meatloaf sandwich on good ol' American white bread, sloshed with some mayo and mustard (and extra pickles if you're me—which you're not).

Ingredients

2 cups fresh breadcrumbs, seasoned or unseasoned
1 cup evaporated milk
1 yellow onion, minced
1 cup sweet pickle relish
2 eggs, beaten
1 tsp. salt
½ tsp. ground black pepper
2 pounds ground beef
½ pound ground pork

Steps

1. Preheat your oven to 350°F. Line the bottom of a 9x5-inch loaf pan with parchment paper.
2. In a large bowl, combine the breadcrumbs, milk, onion, and relish.
3. In a small bowl, whisk the eggs.

4. Stir in the eggs, salt, pepper, ground beef, and ground pork.
5. Using your hands, blend everything very well.
6. Spoon the mixture into the prepared loaf pan.
7. Place into the oven and bake 2 hours or until it reaches at least 160°F on a meat thermometer.
8. Remove from the oven and let cool in the pan 10 minutes.
9. Slice and enjoy.

Swiss Steak

(Serves 4)

My first introduction to Swiss Steak was when I was about eight or nine years of age. The person who introduced me to Swiss Steak, you all remember. Her name was Julia Child, and she made it on her PBS cooking show. I have never been the same since, and I thank her memory every day.

To answer the question you are thinking, yes, Swiss Steak is indeed Swiss in nature. It is actually a very old way of preparing a piece of beef that is braised in a tomato mixture. If you were to dine on this dish in Switzerland, it would probably be listed on the menu as "roast mincemeat." To properly prepare Swiss Steak does take a few steps, but it is rather simple and very delicious.

The best cut of beef for Swiss Steak is a simple cut called "round steak." You can find this in any market with a butcher. It is rather common and decently priced because it can be rather tough in texture if not properly prepared. I would be remiss if I didn't tell you that most diners of the past who prepared this dish actually used a formed ground beef (hamburger)—yeah, not too appetizing.

Ingredients

3-pound round steak, pounded to ½-inch thickness (your butcher can do this for you)

½ cup flour

½ tsp. salt

¼ tsp. ground black pepper

6 Roma tomatoes, chopped

3 cloves garlic, minced

1 tsp. Worcestershire sauce

1 tsp. dried mustard

1 Tbs. brown sugar

½ tsp. celery salt

1 Tbs. rendered bacon fat

1 yellow onion, minced

1 sweet red bell pepper, cored, seeded, and minced

Steps

1. Preheat your oven to 350°F.
2. Slice the beef into serving portions.
3. In a shallow bowl, whisk the flour, salt, and pepper.
4. Dredge (coat) the beef in the seasoned flour. Set the meat aside.
5. Into a food processor, combine the tomatoes, garlic, Worcestershire sauce, mustard, brown sugar, and celery salt and puree. Set aside.
6. In a large sauté pan or skillet, melt the bacon fat over medium heat.
7. Add the beef and brown on all sides.
8. Add the pureed tomato mixture, along with the onion and bell pepper, into the pan.
9. Place into the oven and cook 90 minutes, stirring occasionally.
10. Serve with cooked wide egg noodles or grilled polenta.

Tamale Pie

(Serves 4)

And here is today's food trivia question: What happens when a gringo cook gets hold of a Mexican dish and tries to make something new? Yes, he/she messes it up and creates something brand new, and thus you have the birth of a diner classic, the fabled Tamale Pie! As it turned out, this is one very tasty mistake.

The original Tamale Pie was really nothing more than a bunch of spicy stuff thrown into a pan and baked—really kind of nasty but tasty. Once a few cooks in some diners started to play with it, it began to resemble something you would be proud to put on a plate (with a salad, of course, always with a salad). There are two known versions of Tamale Pie: hot and regular. You will find the hot kind in many eateries throughout the great American Southwest. The regular you will find most other places.

To make a true Tamale Pie, you make the meat mixture separate from the cornmeal mixture. With that noted, this recipe will be in two parts.

For the meat mixture
1 pound ground beef (hamburger)
1 yellow onion, chopped
1 sweet red bell pepper, chopped
4 cloves garlic, minced
1 cup fresh sweet corn kernels
2 tomatoes, chopped
½ cup beef stock
2 jalapeño peppers, stemmed, seeded, and minced
1 Tbs. chili powder
2 tsp. ground cumin
1 tsp. salt
1 tsp. dried oregano, crumbled

Steps
1. In a large sauté pan or skillet over medium heat, combine the ground beef, onion, bell pepper, and garlic and cook 7 minutes. Remove and discard any excess fat.
2. Stir in the corn, tomatoes, beef stock, and jalapeño peppers and cook 5 minutes.

3. Stir in the chili powder, cumin, salt, and oregano and simmer 20 minutes.
4. Preheat your oven to 350°F.

For the cornmeal

2 cups beef stock
1 cup yellow cornmeal
1 tsp. chili powder
½ tsp. salt
1 egg, beaten
½ cup grated cheddar cheese

Steps

1. In a large saucepan, bring the beef stock to a boil over high heat.
2. Gradually whisk in the cornmeal until thickened.
3. Lower the heat to low. Stir in the chili powder and salt and cook, while stirring, 10 minutes.
4. Remove the pan from the heat and vigorously stir in the egg.
5. Spoon the cornmeal over the meat mixture and even out.
6. Top the dish with the grated cheese.
7. Place skillet into the oven and bake 30 minutes.
8. Remove from the oven and let cool slightly before serving.

Texas Fried Chicken

(Serves 4)

In Texas, they say they do everything big. After you have munched on a few pieces of Texas Fried Chicken, you might fully understand what they mean. This is fried chicken with big flavor, a crunchy coating, and very moist meat. Serve this with some biscuits and gravy and give a big "YEEHAW!"

Who do so many Southern-oriented fried chicken dishes include buttermilk? Buttermilk is a cultured milk which features a high point of acidity (lactic acid), and thus, it is not only a natural tenderizer but it can also permeate the skin of fowl (chicken). Of course, it is also one of the more popular dairy products in the South. Once you start to venture West or East, fried chicken is usually just dredged (coated) with a seasoned flour.

This Texas Fried Chicken is a little different than most other fried chickens. Usually, the initial fry time does not require a lid on the pan. With Texas Fried Chicken, you put a lid on the pan for the first round of frying. Yep, leave it to Texans to have to be different.

Ingredients

3 cups buttermilk
2 tsp. hot sauce
2 tsp. salt
2 tsp. ground black pepper
1 chicken, with skin, cut into serving pieces
1 cup corn oil
1 cup flour
1 tsp. chili powder
1 Tbs. ground cumin

Steps

1. In a large bowl, whisk the buttermilk, hot sauce, salt, and pepper.
2. Place the chicken in the buttermilk, cover, and chill overnight.
3. Remove the bowl from the refrigerator and let sit at room temperature for 60 minutes.
4. In a large sauté pan or skillet, bring the oil to 300°F on a deep-fry thermometer.
5. In a ziplock bag, combine the flour, chili powder, and cumin.
6. Dredge (coat) the chicken in the seasoned flour.

7. Carefully place the chicken, skin-side down, in the oil.

8. Reduce the heat to medium, cover, and fry the chicken 15 minutes.

9. Reduce the heat a little lower (just above low). Turn the chicken over and fry 15 minutes without the cover.

10. Remove the chicken to a paper towel–lined plate.

11. Let the chicken cool slightly before serving.

Whiskey Ribs

(Serves 4)

You might be surprised to know this is the only rib dish in this book, and the reason is rather simple. When it comes to rib dishes made famous in diners, truck stops, roadside eateries, and the like, they really didn't do anything special. They plopped some ribs in the oven and then slathered them in a sauce. Nothing special. The good ribs—and the ribs you went out to eat—were at the "shacks." Then there came Whiskey Ribs in the Memphis area, and things started to change.

As you might expect, there is whiskey in these ribs. Matter of fact, there is a lot of whiskey in these ribs. The ribs are not only marinated in the whiskey, but the whiskey is also used for the sauce. With this in mind, remember something very important. It is not true that all alcohol burns off when cooked.

The only ribs allowable by law for this dish are beef ribs. I am almost serious. Whiskey and beef are actually a wonderful combination, and even better, whiskey is a natural meat tenderizer. And yes, you can substitute bourbon for the whiskey.

Ingredients

⅓ cup whiskey

¼ cup soy sauce

2 Tbs. molasses

1 white onion, minced

3 Tbs. dark spicy mustard

1 Tbs. Worcestershire sauce

4 pounds beef ribs

Steps

1. In a large shallow bowl, whisk all the ingredients, except the ribs, until blended.

2. Place the ribs in the marinade, turn over a few times to coat, and chill overnight.

3. Preheat your broiler or grill.

4. Place the ribs on a large broiling pan (or on the grill) and broil (or grill) 10 minutes per side or to desired doneness.

5. Place the marinade in a small pot and bring to a boil over high heat and let boil 5 minutes (it will thicken).

6. After the ribs have broiled (or grilled) five minutes, baste them with the marinade.

7. Remove the ribs to a serving platter and enjoy.

America's Gravies

Classic Sauces

Brown Gravy

(Makes about 1 cup)

Ingredients

2 Tbs. rendered bacon fat
3 Tbs. flour
¼ tsp. salt
⅛ tsp. ground black pepper
1½ cups water
2 Tbs. Worcestershire sauce

Steps

1. In a small skillet, melt the bacon fat over medium heat.

2. Stir in the flour, salt, and pepper and cook a few minutes until it darkens in color.

3. Whisk in the water and Worcestershire sauce until smooth and bring to a simmer.

4. Reduce the heat to low and cook 5 minutes while whisking.

5. Pour into a gravy boat or bowl and serve.

Chicken Gravy

(Makes about 2 cups)

Ingredients

¼ cup drippings from fried chicken
¼ cup flour
½ tsp. salt
¼ tsp. ground black pepper
2 cups milk
1 Tbs. minced parsley

Steps

1. In a medium skillet over medium heat, whisk the drippings, flour, salt, and pepper until smooth and cook a few minutes until it turns golden in color.

2. Whisk in the milk and parsley and bring to a boil.

3. Reduce the heat to low and cook 3 minutes while whisking.

4. Pour into a gravy boat or bowl and serve.

Chicken Fried Steak Gravy

(Makes about 1 cup)

Ingredients

2 Tbs. rendered bacon fat
2 Tbs. flour
½ tsp. salt
¼ tsp. ground black pepper
1 cup milk

Steps

1. In a medium skillet, melt the bacon fat over medium heat.

2. Whisk in the flour, salt, and pepper until smooth.

3. Whisk in the milk until smooth.

4. Reduce the heat to low and keep whisking until you have a thick and smooth gravy.

5. Pour into a gravy boat or bowl and serve.

Mushroom Gravy

(Makes about 1½ cups)

Ingredients

2 Tbs. rendered bacon fat
1 cup sliced mushrooms
2 Tbs. flour
1 cup beef stock
1 tsp. Worcestershire sauce
½ tsp. salt
¼ tsp. ground black pepper

Steps

1. In a medium skillet, melt the bacon fat over medium heat.

2. Stir in the mushrooms and cook 5 minutes.

3. Stir in the flour and cook 1 minute.

4. Whisk in the beef stock, Worcestershire sauce, salt, and pepper until smooth.

5. Reduce the heat to a simmer and cook, while stirring, for 5 minutes.

6. Pour into a gravy boat or bowl and serve.

Orange Sauce

(Makes about 1 cup)

Ingredients

1 Tbs. rendered bacon fat
1 scallion (green onion), minced
1 cup chicken stock
4 strips orange zest
¼ cup dry white wine
2 Tbs. orange juice
¼ tsp. ground paprika
2 tsp. cornstarch
2 Tbs. water

Steps

1. In a medium skillet, melt the bacon fat over medium heat.

2. Add the scallion and cook 2 minutes.

3. Stir in the stock and orange zest and bring to a boil.

4. Reduce the heat to a simmer and cook 10 minutes.

5. With a slotted spoon, remove the orange zest.

6. Stir in the wine, orange juice, and paprika and cook 2 minutes.

7. In a small bowl, whisk the cornstarch and water.

8. Whisk the cornstarch mixture into the gravy until it comes to a boil.

9. Boil 1 minute while whisking.

10. Pour into a gravy boat or bowl and serve.

Sausage Gravy

(Makes about 3 cups)

Ingredients

¼ pound ground pork or sausage meat
¼ cup butter
⅓ cup flour
3½ cups milk
½ tsp. salt
½ tsp. ground black pepper

Steps

1. In a medium skillet, brown the sausage over medium heat.

2. Remove the sausage from the pan and keep 1 Tbs. of the rendered fat in the pan.

3. Stir the butter into the rendered sausage fat until melted.

4. Whisk in the flour and cook 1 minute.

5. Whisk in the milk until smooth.

6. Whisk in the salt and pepper and keep whisking until the sauce has thickened.

7. Stir in the sausage and cook 1 minute.

8. Pour into a gravy boat or bowl and serve.

Tomato Gravy

(Makes about 1½ cups)

Ingredients

2 Tbs. rendered bacon fat
3 Tbs. flour
½ tsp. salt
¼ tsp. ground black pepper
½ cup tomato juice
1 cup water

Steps

1. In a medium skillet, melt the rendered bacon fat over medium heat.

2. Whisk in the flour, salt, and pepper until smooth.

3. Whisk in the tomato juice and water until smooth.

4. Lower the heat and cook 5 minutes while whisking.

5. Pour into a gravy boat or bowl and serve.

All-American Desserts

Cakes, Pies, Brownies, and More

All-American Apple Pie

(Makes 1 pie)

*There is an adage that we have all used, and it goes like this: "American as apple pie."
It is sort of a folksy adage, and it is also totally false. Apple pie is actually European in
nature . . . but it is American by the grace of God!*

   *I do not believe there is a diner or any type of roadside eatery that does not have apple
pie on their dessert menu, and if there is, walk out and never go back. For whatever
reason, there is something about a warm slice of apple pie that makes the heart sing and
the lips tremble. It doesn't matter if it is topped with vanilla ice cream, a slab of cheddar
cheese, or a bourbon-whiskey sauce, apple pie the definition of "dessert."*

   *I think most families have their tried-and-true recipe for apple pie. When it comes to
the diners, cafés, and other such eateries, they usually rely on simplicity (since most
are actually homemade), and in the case of apple pie, simple is often the best. The one
question which always arises with apple pie is: What apple should I use? The answer is
simple: whatever apple is your favorite. Most diners and the like will use an assortment. If
I want a little tartness, I will use Granny Smith. If I want a little more natural sweetness,
I will use Braeburn. If I have more than one type at the house, I will use them all.*

   *You can find the pie crust recipe I use for all my pies on page 276. This All-American
Apple Pie needs both a bottom and top crust.*

Ingredients
4 pounds Braeburn apples, cored, peeled, and thinly sliced
¼ cup flour
½ cup sugar
1 Tbs. lemon juice
½ tsp. ground cinnamon
1 pre-baked pie crust bottom (page 276)
1 unbaked pie crust top (page 276)
1 Tbs. butter, chilled and diced
1 egg
1 Tbs. heavy cream

Steps
1. In a large bowl, toss the apples with the flour, sugar, lemon juice, and cinnamon.
2. Let the apples rest 30 minutes.
3. Preheat your oven to 425°F.

4. Spoon the apples into the pre-baked bottom crust, mounding towards the center.

5. Dot the top of the apples with the butter.

6. Place the unbaked top crust over the pie. Press the edges together to seal the crust.

7. In a small bowl, beat the egg and heavy cream together.

8. Brush the top crust with the egg mixture and then make a few slashes in the crust to act as vents to release the steam that will build up while baking.

9. Place into the oven and bake 15 minutes.

10. Reduce the heat to 350°F and bake 30 minutes.

11. Make a foil tent over the pie and bake an additional 30 minutes.

12. Remove the pie from the oven and let cool on a wire rack.

Apple Brown Betty

(Serves 4)

A little less than one hundred years after America became a country, one if its most beloved desserts was created. The year was 1864, and for the very first time, the recipe for Apple Brown Betty was published. It was obviously created by a lady named Betty who almost, but not quite, burned the dish!

In recent years, it seems as if Apple Brown Betty has lost a significant amount of its popularity. You very seldom see it on menus or served at family dinners. This is truly unfortunate as it is very easy to make and always tastes wonderful, no matter what type of apple you might use to make it. It is also a great way to use stale bread as one of the major components of Apple Brown Betty is breadcrumbs!

As far as what apple goes best with Apple Brown Betty, any apple which retains its texture under heat will work fine. The original dish always featured a red apple. I like to use a Granny Smith, which is a little tarter. The only type of apple you really want to stay away from is a softer variety, such as a Golden Delicious.

Ingredients

4 large red apples, cored, peeled, and thinly sliced
¼ cup brown sugar
¼ cup sugar
1 Tbs. apple cider vinegar
1 tsp. vanilla
½ tsp. ground cinnamon
2 cups dried breadcrumbs
½ cup butter, melted

Steps

1. Preheat your oven to 375°F. Lightly oil or butter a 1-quart baking dish.
2. Place the apples into a large bowl and toss them with both sugars, vinegar, vanilla, and cinnamon.
3. In a medium bowl, stir the breadcrumbs and melted butter.
4. Sprinkle half of the breadcrumbs on the bottom of the baking dish.
5. Layer the apples over the breadcrumbs.
6. Sprinkle the remaining breadcrumbs over the apples.

7. Place a cover on the dish.
8. Place into the oven and bake 45 minutes.
9. Remove the cover and bake an additional 20 minutes.
10. Remove from the oven and let cool on a wire rack.
11. Serve warm and enjoy.

Apple Cobbler

(Serves 4)

I love cobblers. As a matter of fact, I would even go so far as to say I am addicted to cobblers. With this noted, until a few years ago when I first devoured an Apple Cobbler from a café in Washington state, I had never heard of an Apple Cobbler. It is like an apple pie without the crust. Top this with some vanilla ice cream and prepare to visit dessert heaven.

Fruit cobblers were originated in England and got their name because the tops of the dessert resembled the cobblestones of the old English streets. The original cobblers had a topping similar to the texture of scones. They came to America with the settlers and became popular with cooks in the South. Though savory cobblers are not usually found in America, they are quite popular throughout Europe.

What differentiates a cobbler from other desserts like a buckle, pandowdy, or Betty? The topping. The topping of a cobbler is a batter and not really a pastry dough (in the strictest terms) or crumbs. The most popular cobblers feature berries and can be quite "juicy" since the berries will secrete their natural juices. An Apple Cobbler has less syrup.

Ingredients

3 Tbs. butter
4 large red apples, cored, peeled, and thinly sliced
½ cup raisins
1¼ cups sugar, divided
1 tsp. ground cinnamon
¼ tsp. ground nutmeg
½ cup melted butter
1 cup flour
2 tsp. baking powder
1 tsp. salt
½ cup milk

Steps

1. Preheat your oven to 350°F.
2. In a large sauté pan or skillet, melt the butter over medium heat.
3. Add the apples and raisins and sauté 5 minutes.
4. Stir in ¼ cup sugar, cinnamon, and nutmeg and cook 2 minutes.

5. Remove the pan from the heat and set aside.

6. Pour the melted butter into a medium baking dish.

7. Spoon the apple mixture into the baking dish.

8. In a medium bowl, whisk the remaining sugar, flour, baking powder, salt, and milk to form a batter.

9. Spread the batter over the apples.

10. Place into the oven and bake 50 minutes.

11. Remove from the oven and let cool slightly before serving.

Apple Coffee Cake

(Makes 1 cake)

If you have never had the American food memory of walking into the kitchen while your mother or grandmother was baking a spice-laced apple cake, you are missing out on a true piece of Americana. Have no fear though, if this has never happened to you, you can change that by making this very simple yet very scrumptious Apple Coffee Cake which has been a hit in diners and cafés since George Washington chopped down his first tree.

So what really is a coffee cake? Does it contain coffee? To answer the last question first, no, a coffee cake does not usually contain coffee. To answer the first question, it is a cake that is usually enjoyed with cup of coffee or tea. It is also a great light dessert which may feature fruit in one way or another, and in this case, that fruit is apple.

When it comes to using apples in a cake or any other baked good where apples are introduced into a batter, obviously the type of apple is important. For this cake, I like to us a Granny Smith apple. I think the slight tartness goes well with the sweetness of the cake.

You will notice something strange when you prepare this cake. You will not have the usual batter. It will be rather thick and crumbly. Fear not, you've done nothing wrong. Due to the fact that the apple will emit all of its juice during the baking process, as the cake bakes, it will essentially create its own batter. Pretty cool, huh?

Ingredients

1 cup flour
1 tsp. baking powder
½ tsp. salt
1 large Granny Smith, cored, peeled, and diced
1 egg, beaten
1 cup sugar
½ cup finely chopped walnuts
¼ cup corn oil
1 tsp. ground cinnamon
¼ tsp. ground nutmeg

Steps

1. Preheat your oven to 350°F. Line the bottom of an 8-inch cake pan with parchment paper.
2. In a medium bowl, whisk the flour, baking powder, and salt.

3. In a large bowl, toss the apples with the egg, sugar, walnuts, oil, cinnamon, and nutmeg.

4. Stir the flour mixture into the apple mixture until well combined.

5. Spoon the mixture into the prepared cake pan and, using your fingers, pat it down into the pan.

6. Place into the oven and bake 45 minutes.

7. Remove from the oven and let the cake cool in the pan 5 minutes.

8. Remove the cake to a cooling rack until ready to serve.

Baked Apples

(Serves 4)

Before we get started, let me say this dish does contain alcohol and a pretty good shot of it.

Baked Apples have been an institution among American desserts for as long as anyone can remember. According to food lore, they were first put upon a dinner table in the Northeast during the winter months. This makes total sense since they truly do warm the cockles of one's heart, and if your threshold for alcohol is low, they might give you a pretty good warm buzz!

What you are going to do with the apples here is first stuff them and then bake them. To stuff apples is quite easy as long as you remember one thing. When you core the apple, you do not want to go all the way through to the bottom. You want to leave the bottom of the apple intact, so the stuffing does not leak out during the baking process. The best way to do this is to core the apple with a small melon-baller or a perforated grapefruit spoon.

The authentic nut stuffing for Baked Apples calls for pecans. Depending on where you are located, pecans can be downright expensive. You can also use walnuts or any soft variety of nut. The best type of apple to use for this dish is one which will hold its shape and texture during the baking process. To be authentic, you would want a larger variety of red apple. If you want a little tartness to go with the sweetness of the nut stuffing, you can use a large variety of Granny Smith.

Ingredients

4 large apples, unpeeled and cored (see note above)
¼ cup sugar
1 Tbs. lemon juice
¼ cup finely chopped pecans or walnuts
1 egg white
½ cup bourbon or whiskey
½ cup boiling water

Steps

1. Preheat your oven to 375°F.
2. Place the apples into an 8-inch baking dish.
3. In a small bowl, stir together the sugar, lemon juice, nuts, and egg white.
4. Fill each of the apples with the nut mixture.

5. Pour the bourbon and boiling water over the apples. Baste the apples with this mixture a few times during the baking process.

6. Place into the oven and bake 45 minutes. The apples should be fork-tender yet not mushy.

7. Remove from the oven and let cool slightly before serving.

8. Have a small bowl or pitcher of the baking juices at the table to drizzle over the apples.

Baked Apple Pudding

(Serves 4)

Rumor has it that Baked Apple Pudding was one of the favorite desserts Martha would fix for George Washington. Since this was just a little before my time, I cannot back this rumor up with firsthand knowledge, but . . . the art of pudding did come to America with the colonists and good ol' George is the founding father of America, so . . .

When puddings were the dessert rage in America during the '50s and '60s, this was one of the more popular kinds sold in diners and roadside eateries. It was also quite popular in American homes during the fall and winter months. Unlike many puddings, this is a very simple and quick pudding to make at home and is pretty much foolproof.

All of the original recipes for Baked Apple Puddings call for a red apple. I think this is because, during the time this dish was being perfected, there weren't that many other varieties available in America. Personally, I think the best apple for this is a Golden Delicious, and the soft texture of the apple will blend wonderfully well in the pudding and give you a perfect texture.

Ingredients

6 Tbs. butter, softened
¼ cup sugar
1 egg, beaten
½ cup flour
½ tsp. baking powder
¼ cup milk
1 large Golden Delicious apple, peeled, cored, and diced
1 tsp. grated ginger

Steps

1. Preheat your oven to 375°F.
2. Lightly butter 4 heat-proof custard cups or large ramekins.
3. In a mixer with the paddle attachment, beat the butter and sugar until light.
4. Beat in the egg, flour, and baking powder until smooth.
5. Beat in the milk until you have a batter.
6. Stir in the apple and ginger.
7. Spoon the mixture into the prepared custard cups.
8. Place into the oven and bake 30 minutes.
9. Remove from the oven and let cool before serving.

Coconut Cream Pie

(Makes 1 pie)

Cream pies are the main ingredient of dreams. They are light, lush, smooth, and delicious. There is something very special about that first forkful of a cream pie when it passes your lips and reaches the destination of your tongue. You savor those first few minutes with absolute rapture . . . and then you pig out!

Coconut Cream Pie—the real deal and not some sludge from the supermarket—actually contains no coconut meat. An actual Coconut Cream Pie gets its flavor from pure coconut milk. The coconut milk is made into a coconut custard and then spooned into a pie crust and chilled to set. It is very easy. During the early days of diners, where Coconut Cream Pie was a favorite, coconut milk was not used due to the expensive price. They instead used an imitation coconut flavoring.

Since this is not a baked pie, you will want to use a pre-baked pie crust. You can find the recipe for ours on page 276, or you can use a good quality store-bought one. You only need a bottom crust. This will make one 9-inch pie.

Ingredients

⅓ cup sugar
¼ cup cornstarch
2 cups coconut milk
5 egg yolks, beaten
¼ cup butter
1 Tbs. vanilla
pre-baked 9-inch bottom pie crust (page 276)

Steps

1. In a medium saucepan over medium heat, whisk the sugar, cornstarch, coconut milk, egg yolks, and butter until it comes to a simmer and thickens to the point of custard.

2. Remove the pan from the heat and whisk in the vanilla.

3. Spoon the custard into a bowl and chill at least 2 hours.

4. Spoon the custard into the pre-baked pie crust and chill until ready to slice and serve.

Banana Cream Pie

(Makes 1 pie)

Cream pies. Americans have loved cream pies since the first pie made its way onto a dessert plate. What's not to love? They have a smooth texture. They have a perfect sweetness. They are easy to make. They pack on the calories . . . oh well, two out of three ain't bad!

When I was a kid, I used to love going into diners and looking at the desserts. They always had them out there where you could see them. One of my favorite desserts to ogle, in general, were the pies—and in particular, the cream pies. I loved how they made little stars with the whipped cream, and they always had one slice sitting there on display. I couldn't wait to finish my meal so I could dive in.

When it comes to cream pies, Americans have always had a hankering for Banana Cream Pie. There is just something we love about that rich creamy texture layered with thin slices of banana. Whereas manufactured cream pies, the ones you buy frozen at the market, always have that disgusting graham cracker crust, the ones at the diners and cafés always had a real crust, and that is the only way a banana cream pie should be enjoyed.

For this pie, you can use a pre-baked 9-inch pie crust or you can make your own with our recipe on page 276.

Ingredients

2 cups half-and-half
½ cup sugar
¼ cup cornstarch
4 egg yolks
1 cup milk
2 Tbs. butter
1 Tbs. vanilla
pre-baked 9-inch pie crust (page 276)
2 bananas, peeled and thinly sliced
maraschino cherries, chopped (optional)

Steps

1. In a medium pot over medium heat, whisk the half-and-half, sugar, and cornstarch and bring to a simmer.

2. In a small bowl, whisk the egg yolks and milk.

3. Whisk the egg yolk mixture into the hot half-and-half mixture and keep whisking until it has thickened to a custard consistency.

4. Remove the pot from the heat and stir in the butter and vanilla.

5. Layer some of the custard over the bottom of the pie crust.

6. Place a layer of banana slices over the custard. Spread another layer of custard over the bananas.

7. Layer the remaining bananas over the custard.

8. Finish the pie with another layer of custard.

9. Place the pie in the refrigerator and chill at least 2 hours before slicing and serving.

10. If desired, garnish with chopped maraschino cherries just before serving.

Blueberry Pie

(Makes 1 pie)

Confession time. I think I may be the last person of my generation to eat Blueberry Pie. I never had a piece of Blueberry Pie until I was in my forties. To be more honest, I never had fresh blueberries until I was in my forties. Why? Well, they just weren't a big thing when I was growing up in San Francisco, and as I got older (and then much older), it just wasn't on my bucket list.

My first slice of Blueberry Pie came in a diner in Topeka, Kansas. The only reason I tried it is because the people I was with said, "Larry, you've got to try the Blueberry Pie." I was in no mood to argue. I tried it. I then ordered another slice. Yep, I became a Blueberry Pie addict. Little orbs of natural sweetness exploding in my mouth with every chew. Yum!

The great thing about Blueberry Pie is the fact that you can make it perfectly with either fresh blueberries or frozen. How cool is that? If you do use the frozen variety, make sure they are individually flash-frozen (it will say so on the package). What you do not want to use (ever) are those things sold in cans as "pie filling"—stay away from those like the plague, which is essentially what they are.

For this pie, you will need a crust (duh!), and you can use a good quality two-part pie crust as Blueberry Pie needs a top crust—or you can use my pie crust recipe, which you will find on page 276.

Ingredients

1¼ cups sugar
2 Tbs. cornstarch
1 tsp. ground cinnamon
5 cups blueberries (if frozen, do NOT defrost)
1 Tbs. lemon juice
2-piece pie crust (pre-baked bottom, unbaked top) (page 276)

Steps

1. Preheat your oven to 450°F.

2. In a large bowl, whisk the sugar, cornstarch, and cinnamon.

3. Fold in the blueberries and lemon juice.

4. Let the blueberries rest 30 minutes.

5. Spoon the blueberries into the pre-baked pie crust, mounding them towards the center. (The blueberries will shrink while baking.)

6. Place the top unbaked crust over the pie and seal the edges.

7. Make four slits in the top crust to act as steam vents.

8. Place into the oven and bake 15 minutes.

9. Reduce the heat to 350°F and cover the edges (rim) of the crust with foil to prevent burning.

10. Bake an additional 40 minutes.

11. Remove the Blueberry Pie from the oven and let cool before slicing and serving.

Brownies

(Makes varying amount, depending on size)

NEWSFLASH! BROWNIES DO NOT COME FROM A BOX! Thank you, I feel so much better now.

If you have never experienced real homemade brownies made from real chocolate or good quality cocoa, you have not yet begun to live. There was a time when these squares of chocolate euphoria, served with a scoop of pure vanilla ice cream, were one of the top diner desserts in this land. Then came along the evil processed food movement, and they seemed to disappear. Brownies are an American tradition and should be brought back to life—and with this recipe, I hope they will be.

For this Brownie recipe, we are going to use a good quality cocoa powder instead of chocolate (yes, there is a difference) because, most of the time, this is how they were made. When it comes to cocoa powder, you do want to stay away from those which are alkalized. You want it as pure as possible. When you combine cocoa powder with melted butter, you essentially get a good quality chocolate—kind of cool, huh?

In the great American Southwest, they still make one of the better Brownies, and the reason is one very simple ingredient that you probably have right in your kitchen right now. It is chili powder. Yes, chili powder. The essence of the chili powder brings out the robustness of the cocoa, and this is a centuries-old trick used by the Aztecs who, arguably, invented chocolate from cocoa.

Ingredients

½ cup melted butter
½ cup cocoa powder
1 cup sugar
2 eggs, beaten
1 Tbs. vanilla
½ cup flour
¼ tsp. salt
¼ tsp. chili powder

Steps

1. Preheat your oven to 350°F. Line the bottom of an 8-inch square cake pan with parchment paper.

2. In a large bowl, whisk the butter, cocoa powder, sugar, eggs, and vanilla until thick and smooth.

3. Stir in the flour, salt, and chili powder just until combined.
4. Spoon into the prepared pan and even out.
5. Place into the oven and bake 25 minutes.
6. Remove from the oven and let cool in the pan 10 minutes.
7. Remove from the pan and cool on a wire rack until ready to slice and serve.

Buttermilk Cake

(Makes 1 cake)

You've got to admire the love affair the South has with buttermilk. If it wasn't for this flavorful addiction, we wouldn't have some of the most flavorful dishes in America. Whether it be frying or baking, when buttermilk is involved, it is going to be Southern and delicious!

One of the most popular cakes you will ever find in the diners of the South is the very simple yet quite flavorful Buttermilk Cake. This cake, with a dense crumb (texture), is usually served with a heavy coating of frosting, and for some reason, that frosting is always pastel-colored (no one has ever told me why). It is usually served as dessert during the lunch hours.

If you are new to baking with buttermilk as an ingredient, you are in for a very important culinary chemistry experiment. Because buttermilk is a cultured product, it interacts with other ingredients (which is why it is often used in biscuits and cornbread). It will naturally lighten a batter or dough and give it a very slight acidic taste.

Ingredients

1½ cups flour
1 tsp. baking powder
¼ tsp. baking soda
½ tsp. ground cinnamon
¼ tsp. salt
½ cup butter, softened
1 cup sugar
2 eggs, beaten
2 Tbs. vanilla
½ cup buttermilk

Steps

1. Preheat your oven to 375°F. Line the bottom of a 9-inch cake pan with parchment paper.
2. In a medium bowl, whisk together the flour, baking powder, baking soda, cinnamon, and salt.
3. In a mixer with the paddle attachment, beat the butter and sugar until smooth.
4. Add the eggs and beat for 5 minutes.

5. Beat in ⅓ cup of the flour mixture.
6. Add the vanilla and buttermilk and beat for 5 minutes.
7. Add the remaining flour and beat just until blended.
8. Spoon into the prepared pan and even out.
9. Place into the oven and bake 30 minutes.
10. Remove from the oven and let cool in the pan 5 minutes.
11. Remove from the pan and let cool on a wire rack.

Buttermilk Cornmeal Shortcake

(Makes 6)

Shortcake! Most Americans only know shortcake when it is piled with strawberries and topped with whipped cream. Though this is indeed a wonderful dessert, when it comes to shortcake, people have a tendency to forget that the star of this dessert should be the actual shortcake, and unfortunately, when it comes to shortcake, you're usually getting . . . crap! A real shortcake is a very delicate pastry!

There are actually two types of shortcake. There is the European style, using flour. Then there is the purely American style, which uses cornmeal. Both are quite good, but the American version, with cornmeal, has a more crunchy texture and marries absolutely perfectly with any kind of berry and will not get soggy with the whipped cream.

Buttermilk Cornmeal Shortcake is actually made like a cookie, meaning it is rolled out and then cut into shape. Once baked, it is quite delicate, so you want to be a little extra careful when removing it from the baking sheet. Since these are made with cornmeal, they will dry out faster than the European shortcakes, so if you're going to have any left over, wrap them in plastic.

Ingredients

2½ cups flour
¾ cup yellow cornmeal
½ cup sugar
1 Tbs. baking powder
6 Tbs. butter, chilled and diced
1 cup buttermilk

Steps

1. Preheat your oven to 425°F. Line a baking sheet with parchment paper or a silicone baking sheet.
2. In a medium bowl, whisk the flour, cornmeal, sugar, and baking powder.
3. Add the butter and, using a pastry blender, cut the butter into the flour mixture until crumbly.
4. Stir in the buttermilk until you have a dough.

5. Place the dough on a floured surface and knead until it comes together.
6. Roll the dough out on a floured surface to a thickness of 1 inch.
7. Using a 2-inch round cookie or biscuit cutter, cut out the shortcakes.
8. Place the shortcakes on the prepared baking sheet.
9. Place into the oven and bake 15 minutes or until golden
10. Remove from the oven and cool on a wire rack.

Buttermilk Crumb Cake

(Makes 1 cake)

Whether it be for breakfast, a noontime snack, or dessert after dinner, you can never top a good crumb cake. So, what really is a crumb cake? It is a cake topped with crumbs—what did you think it was?

If you have ever had an actual crumb cake, then you are well aware of the fact that the texture is somewhat different than a regular type of cake. Whereas a cake, such as the famed yellow cake, has a rather dense texture, a crumb cake is usually lighter and airier. Why is this? Thank you for asking! It is due to the fact that an actual crumb cake is made with buttermilk, and the buttermilk has a tendency to cause a chemical reaction with the other ingredients, especially baking powder and baking soda.

Crumb cakes have always been a popular treat served at Sunday church gatherings. They also have an important part in the history of diners and cafés due to their easy preparation, the fact they can be served at all hours, and their slight sweetness. Everyone should have at least one crumb cake in their baking repertoire.

Ingredients

3 cups flour
2 cups brown sugar
½ cup butter, softened
2 tsp. ground nutmeg
2 eggs, beaten
1 cup buttermilk
1 tsp. baking powder
½ tsp. baking soda
¼ cup finely chopped pecans or walnuts

Steps

1. Preheat your oven to 350°F degrees. Line the bottom of a 13x9-inch cake pan with parchment paper.

2. In a mixer with the paddle attachment, beat the flour, brown sugar, butter, and nutmeg until it is crumbly.

3. Remove 1 cup of the mixture and set aside (this will be the topping).

4. Into the mixer, beat in the eggs, buttermilk, baking powder, and baking soda to make a batter.

5. Spoon the batter into the prepared pan.
6. Sprinkle the top of the batter with the topping and the nuts.
7. Place into the oven and bake 45 minutes.
8. Remove from the oven and let cool in the pan 5 minutes.
9. Remove from the pan and cool on a wire rack.

Buttermilk Pound Cake

(Makes 1 cake)

I am addicted to pound cake. Until the time the Betty Ford Clinic comes up with a cure for this food ailment of mine, you will always find a pound cake somewhere in my kitchen, and the crumbs from said cake somewhere on my face. Judge me; I don't care! So, what is a pound cake? Well, originally it was a pound of butter, a pound of sugar, a pound of flour, and a pound of eggs. No, I have no idea how it got its name.

This pound cake is a little different than many others. This pound cake used to be quite popular in diners and cafés not so much as a dessert in itself but because it was one of the better cakes to serve with fresh fruit and either ice cream or whipped cream. The reason it was not served on its own too often is that it is not as sweet as your typical cake.

Most of the time this pound cake is made in a Bundt-style cake pan (which can be found at any kitchenware store). I tend to be a rebel and make it in a loaf pan. Why? Because I like it better, it slices better, and I don't want to fight with it to get it out of the pan!

Ingredients

1 cup butter, softened
2 cups sugar
4 eggs, beaten
1 Tbs. vanilla
3 cups flour
½ tsp. baking powder
½ tsp. baking soda
¼ tsp. salt
1 cup buttermilk, divided

Steps

1. Preheat your oven to 325°F. Lightly oil and flour a 12-cup Bundt cake pan.
2. In a mixer with the paddle attachment, beat the butter and sugar 5 minutes.
3. Beat in the eggs, one at a time, along with the vanilla, and beat 5 minutes.
4. In a large bowl, whisk the flour, baking powder, baking soda, and salt.
5. Into the mixer, add half of the flour mixture and beat just until combined.
6. Add half the buttermilk and beat until smooth.

7. Add the remaining flour mixture and beat just until combined.
8. Add the remaining buttermilk and beat 5 minutes.
9. Spoon the batter into the prepared Bundt pan.
10. Place into the oven and bake 70 minutes or until done.
11. Remove from the oven and let cool in the pan 10 minutes.
12. Remove from the pan and cool on a wire rack.

Cinnamon Apple Cake

(Makes 1 cake)

Remember that sorta apple-and-spice cake your mother or grandmother used to make? She probably dusted the top with powdered sugar, and when you got home from school, you couldn't wait to sink your teeth into a piece. Yeah, that cake. Well, that cake used to be rather popular lunch fare in some diners, and no, it didn't really contain apples in the strictest sense. It contained applesauce (usually bought in huge cans).

For many people, this is one of those desserts which falls under the category of "comfort foods." Luckily, it is also a cake that is foolproof to make and takes very little time (as far as cakes are concerned). So you see, you really have no excuse not to relive one of your favorite flavorful childhood memories!

When it comes to applesauce, they are all pretty much the same. I would recommend buying the "natural" variety as it will not have any extra sugar or spices in it. You don't need those as you will be adding the real stuff when you prepare Cinnamon Apple Cake.

Ingredients

2 cups flour
2 cups sugar
½ cup butter, softened
2 eggs, beaten
1½ cups applesauce
1½ tsp. baking soda
½ tsp. baking powder
1½ tsp. ground cinnamon
1 tsp. vanilla

Steps

1. Preheat your oven to 350°F. Line the bottom of a 9-inch cake pan with parchment paper.
2. In a mixer with the paddle attachment, combine all of the ingredients and beat for 5 minutes.
3. Spoon the batter into the prepared pan and even out.
4. Place into the oven and bake 35 minutes.

5. Remove from the oven and let the cake cool in the pan 5 minutes.

6. Remove the cake to a wire rack and cool until ready to slice and serve.

Cherry Pie

(Makes 1 pie)

Of course, you can go to your local supermarket and buy a frozen cherry pie. Plop it in the oven and then, about forty minutes or so later, put a fork of it to your mouth. You can also go to DOW Chemical and lick one of their hoses. I really do not know which would be more nutritious! C'mon, pie-making is an American art form and should be celebrated thusly (albeit they were not originated in the land of red, white, and blue).

You'll see quite a few pies in this chapter, and you will notice they all have one thing in common: the crust. All diners and cafés used one basic crust. It was a lard-based crust because lard was readily available and cheap (lard is rendered animal fat). Things started to change when lard got some bad press, and the crust was changed to a butter-based crust. You can use either with no problem, albeit lard is now much more expensive. Lard will give you a flakier crust; butter a more flavorful crust. You can find our recipe for pie crust (using butter) on page 276, and it is the pie crust we use for all our pies (sweet and savory).

And now for the cherries. What should you use? To prepare cherries for a cherry pie does take some time if you were to do it naturally. Not too many people have time for this, so you can do two things. You can use the canned cherry pie filling (yuck!), which is what most of the cooks at the diners used. On the other hand, you can use fresh or organic canned cherries and follow the directions I give you with this recipe.

Ingredients
6 cups cherries (make sure they are pitted)
3 Tbs. tapioca pearls (no, not the pudding)
¾ cup sugar (more if using sour cherries)
¼ tsp. almond extract
unbaked pie crust, top and bottom (page 276)

Steps
1. In a large bowl, combine the cherries, tapioca pearls, sugar, and almond extract.
2. Let the cherries macerate (sit) 30 minutes.
3. Meanwhile, preheat your oven to 350°F.
4. Spoon the cherry mixture into the pie crust.
5. Place the top crust over the cherries and seal the edges.
6. Make four slits in the top crust to act as steam vents.
7. Place into the oven and bake 55 minutes.
8. Remove from the oven and let the pie cool on a wire rack.

Country Cherry Cobbler

(Serves 4)

Whereas cobblers are an English tradition (thus the name, which came about because the topping resembled the cobblestone streets of England), this version is purely American. The difference is the way in which the cobbler is constructed. I guess you can say it is put together backwards. Who cares! It tastes good and is a perfect way to end your meal.

Personally, I love to make this cobbler with sour cherries, and you can find some very good organic canned ones in your market. This is also a great dessert to make during the height of cherry season with ripe cherries (pitted, of course), either whole or halved. The one thing you do not ever want to use is that canned stuff called "cherry pie filling." If you're not a fan of cherries, you can use this very same recipe with other berries, except strawberries.

The "crust" or topping for the cobbler is one of my favorites. Many times, an American cobbler will feature buttermilk. This one does not. If you are a fan of buttermilk, you can substitute buttermilk for the milk in this recipe.

Ingredients

½ cup butter
1 egg, beaten
1 tsp. vanilla
1 cup milk
1 cup sugar
1 cup flour
1 tsp. baking powder
1 tsp. salt
4 cups cherries (pitted)

Steps

1. Preheat your oven to 375°F.
2. In a medium sauté pan or skillet, melt the butter over medium heat.
3. In a medium bowl, whisk the egg, vanilla, milk, sugar, flour, baking powder, and salt to form a batter.
4. Pour the batter into the pan and let it naturally spread out.
5. Place the cherries atop the batter.
6. Place into the oven and bake 45 minutes or until golden. You will notice the batter rises to form the top "crust."
7. Remove from the oven and let cool before serving.

Country Inn Crumb Cake

(Makes 1 cake)

If you have never taken a lazy Sunday drive on a warm summer or spring day to visit the country inns in your area, you are missing out on not only a fun day but oftentimes a very delicious day. Country inns are known for their, usually, fantastic American fare, and more often than not, they are rather historical. It is a great way to spend the day with family and make some wonderful memories.

I think a great way to start any day is with a freshly brewed cup of coffee and something to satiate the sweet tooth, so rather logically one of my favorite ways to enjoy a breakfast is with a fresh crumb cake—and they don't get much better that Country Inn Crumb Cake. This is one of those rare crumb cakes that is rather light in texture and has a simply perfect amount of sweetness. It will also make your kitchen smell wonderful.

Within the batter of this crumb cake is oil. When oil is added to any type of batter, it will give you a much more delicate texture—even more so than butter, which is used more for a rich flavor and its fat. In the case of this crumb cake, the butter is saved for the topping. Try this Country Inn Crumb Cake just once, and I have a feeling it will soon become a staple in your baking repertoire.

Ingredients

1½ cups flour
1 cup sugar
1 Tbs. baking powder
½ cup vegetable oil
¼ cup milk
1 Tbs. vanilla
3 eggs, beaten
⅓ cup brown sugar
2 tsp. ground cinnamon
¼ cup butter, chilled and diced

Steps

1. Preheat your oven to 350°F. Line the bottom of an 8-inch cake pan with parchment paper.
2. In a large bowl, whisk the flour, sugar, and baking powder.
3. In a medium bowl, whisk the oil, milk, vanilla, and eggs.

4. Stir the milk mixture into the flour mixture just until it is moistened.
5. Spoon the batter into the prepared pan.
6. Sprinkle the top with the brown sugar and cinnamon.
7. Dot the top with the butter.
8. Place into the oven and bake 50 minutes.
9. Remove from the oven and let cool in the pan 10 minutes.
10. Remove from the pan and cool on a wire rack.

Cranberry and Banana Bread

(Makes 1 loaf)

I'm sure everyone who loves bananas has had banana bread. It is a classic American dessert bread. During the fall months when cranberries are in season, cranberry bread is very popular and a favorite food gift to give during the holidays. Somewhere along the line, probably in the Midwest or Northeast, some genius decided to put them together, and for this, we should all be grateful.

In a lot of smaller cafés throughout America, dessert breads are quite popular, and the reason is quite simple. Most cafés are rather quaint (small), with small staffs and limited budgets (and great food). Due to this, they rely on simplicity, and there are not many desserts simpler than a dessert bread. Dessert breads are also very versatile. They can be a dessert by themselves or made a little fancy with some fruit and/or cream.

When Cranberry and Banana Bread was first created, it was with fresh cranberries and was a seasonal dessert bread. As dehydration became more popular, dried cranberries started to be used, and the dessert became a regular year-round staple. This also makes for a great breakfast when it is toasted and then slathered with some sweet cream butter.

Ingredients

⅔ cup sugar
½ cup butter, softened
2 eggs, beaten
1 cup mashed bananas
1 Tbs. lemon juice
2 cups flour
1 tsp. baking powder
½ tsp. baking soda
½ tsp. salt
½ cup dried cranberries
1 cup finely chopped walnuts

Steps

1. Preheat your oven to 350°F. Line the bottom of a 9x5-inch loaf pan with parchment paper.
2. In a mixer with the paddle attachment, beat the sugar, butter, and eggs until smooth.
3. Stir in the bananas and lemon juice.
4. In a medium bowl, whisk the flour, baking powder, baking soda, and salt.
5. Stir the flour mixture into the batter.
6. Fold in the cranberries and nuts.
7. Spoon the batter into the prepared loaf pan.
8. Place into the oven and bake 60 minutes.
9. Remove from the oven and let cool in the pan 10 minutes.
10. Remove from the pan and let cool on a wire rack until ready to slice and serve.

Depression Cake

(Makes 1 cake)

In 1930s America, there was a devastating occurrence referred to as the Great Depression. For details of this period in American history, please refer to an encyclopedia; after all, this is just a cookbook, but . . . apparently this cake originated during this tragic time.

Aside from the fact that this cake was created during the Depression, it is also a cake that ensured many food products didn't go to waste, much like the "junk cake" that uses products about to be spoiled. When spices were in the kitchen and about to lose their pungency, this is one of the dishes that would be made. It is very much like the beloved spice cake, albeit includes nuts and a slightly different method of putting the cake together.

You might notice something strange about this cake. It features no eggs. It features no dairy. It is vegan! You might think this is quite out of the ordinary for this time in American history, but it makes sense when you think about it. During the Depression, eggs and dairy cost money, and the items used in this cake could usually be found in the typical kitchen/pantry without having to incur any additional costs.

Ingredients

1 cup brown sugar
⅓ cup corn oil
1 tsp. ground cinnamon
¼ tsp. ground cloves
2 cups raisins
⅛ tsp. salt
1 cup water
2 cups flour
½ tsp. baking powder
1 tsp. baking soda
3 Tbs. hot water
1 cup finely chopped walnuts

Steps

1. Preheat your oven to 350°F. Line the bottom of an 8- or 9-inch cake pan (round or square) with parchment paper.

2. In a medium saucepan over medium heat, stir the brown sugar, oil, cinnamon, cloves, raisins, salt, and water. Bring the mixture to a boil.

3. Reduce the heat to a simmer and cook 5 minutes.
4. Remove the saucepan from the heat and let cool to room temperature.
5. In a large bowl, whisk the flour, baking powder, and baking soda.
6. Stir in the cooled sugar mixture, hot water, and nuts to form a batter.
7. Spoon the batter into the prepared cake pan.
8. Place into the oven and bake 45 minutes or until done.
9. Remove from the oven and let cool in the pan 10 minutes.
10. Remove from the pan and let cool on a wire rack.

Devil's Food Cake

(Makes 1 cake)

Stop right there. No, a Devil's Food Cake is not the opposite of an Angel's Food Cake, albeit one is dark and the other is light. Now that we have that out of the way, what is the difference between a Devil's Food Cake and a chocolate cake? Good question with a simple answer. The amount of chocolate. An authentic Devil's Food Cake is very dark (almost black) while a chocolate cake is brown. There is one other difference, and it really is the important one. A Devil's Food Cake has a dense and deep texture whereas a typical chocolate cake is . . . well, just a cake.

Devil's Food Cake may be the most popular dessert of all time at diners and cafés. They were usually two layers and featured a dark fudge frosting. They looked majestic when they came to your table, and if you were really lucky, there was a scoop or two of freshly churned chocolate ice cream on the side. A good and proper Devil's Food Cake dessert could put you into sugar nirvana!

Since we are making this Devil's Food Cake the authentic way, you will need to melt some chocolate, and in the steps, we will share with you the easiest and safest way to do this. You will want to use a good quality bittersweet chocolate with a cocoa index of at least sixty percent. And remember when your mom would tell you, don't open the oven door when you're baking a cake 'cause it will fall? She was right. Don't do it!

By the way, this makes one cake (or layer). If you want to make a double-layer cake, double the ingredients and use two pans. Simple enough!

Ingredients

1 tsp. baking soda
½ cup buttermilk
½ cup boiling water
4 ounces bittersweet chocolate
½ cup butter, softened
2 cups brown sugar
3 egg yolks, beaten
1 tsp. vanilla
½ cup strong black coffee
2 cups flour, divided

Steps

1. Preheat your oven to 350°F. Line the bottom of a 9-inch cake pan with parchment paper.

2. In a small bowl, whisk the baking soda in the buttermilk.

3. In a small bowl, pour the boiling water over the chocolate and stir until the chocolate has melted.

4. In a mixer with the paddle attachment, beat the butter, brown sugar, and eggs until light and fluffy.

5. Stir in the chocolate, vanilla, and coffee.

6. Stir in half of the flour.

7. Stir in the buttermilk until smooth.

8. Stir in the remaining flour until combined.

9. Spoon the batter into the prepared cake pan.

10. Place into the oven and bake 35 minutes.

11. Remove from the oven and let cool in the pan 10 minutes.

12. Remove from the pan and let cool on a wire rack. The cake must be totally cooled before frosting it.

Drunk Apple Betty

(Serves 4)

So, you might be wondering, what is the difference between Apple Brown Betty and Drunk Apple Betty? Quite obviously, Betty was drunk when she made this version. Okay, maybe not, but after she ate this version, she might have had a little buzz. The main difference is that this one features bourbon—and not just a little touch of the amber liquid but a full half cup!

A little less than one hundred years after America became a country, one of its most beloved desserts was created. The year was 1864, and for the very first time, the recipe for Apple Brown Betty was published. It was obviously created by a lady named Betty who almost, but not quite, burned the dish! Some years later, someone added bourbon to the recipe, and for this, we should all be thankful.

In recent years, it seems as if Apple Brown Betty has lost a significant amount of its popularity. You very seldom see it on menus or served at family dinners. This is truly unfortunate as it is very easy to make and always tastes wonderful, no matter what type of apple you might use to make it. It is also a great way to use stale bread as one of the major components of Apple Brown Betty is breadcrumbs!

Yes, you can substitute whiskey for the bourbon. You can also—and I have done this—use a spiced rum. No matter what the booze may be, it is good!

Ingredients

2½ cups dried breadcrumbs
½ cup butter, melted
2 pounds apples, peeled, cored, and thinly sliced
¾ cup brown sugar
¼ tsp. ground cinnamon
½ cup bourbon (or whiskey)

Steps

1. Preheat your oven to 375°F. Lightly oil or butter the bottom of a baking dish.
2. In a medium bowl, toss the breadcrumbs in the melted butter.
3. In a large bowl, toss the apples, sugar, and cinnamon.
4. Sprinkle one third of the crumbs over the bottom of the prepared baking dish.
5. Layer half of the apples atop the crumbs.
6. Sprinkle another third of the crumbs over the apples.

7. Layer the remaining apples over the crumbs.
8. Sprinkle the remaining crumbs over the apples.
9. Pour the bourbon over all.
10. Cover the top of the baking dish with foil.
11. Place into the oven and bake 25 minutes.
12. Remove the foil and bake an additional 45 minutes.
13. Remove the Drunk Apple Betty from the oven and let cool before serving.

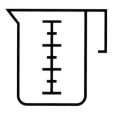

Maple Bourbon Cake

(Makes 1 cake)

There are certain parts of this great land where, no matter what you eat, there is going to be booze involved. I, for one, am thankful for these places! There is just something about eating food laden with booze which makes me feel good, and when you're a kid (as I was once upon a time), it makes you feel as if you're getting away with something. And in a very real way, you are; you're getting away with eating some damn good food.

Cakes are an American tradition, albeit it not originating here, and the chances are very strong that one of the first desserts ever made on American soil was a cake. Mind you, there is no proof to back that statement up, but then again, there is no proof to disclaim it either. Maple cake is, however, an American original, and this version is not only very simple to make at home, it is almost foolproof. By the way, if you want to make this without the bourbon or whiskey, just use a little more maple syrup.

On the subject of maple syrup, NEVER use that stuff referred to as "pancake syrup." It is not maple syrup, and it has no maple in it. It is a flavored corn syrup and very bad for you. Real maple syrup is a little expensive, but the flavor and aroma are well worth the price.

Ingredients

½ cup butter, softened
½ cup sugar
2 eggs, beaten
2½ tsp. baking powder
2 cups flour
½ tsp. salt
¼ tsp. ground nutmeg
½ cup maple syrup
½ cup bourbon (or whiskey)
1½ cups finely chopped pecans (or walnuts)

Steps

1. Preheat your oven to 350°F. Line the bottom of a 9-inch cake pan with parchment paper.

2. In a mixer with the paddle attachment, beat the butter and sugar until light and fluffy.

3. Add the eggs and beat for 5 minutes at medium speed.
4. In a medium bowl, whisk the baking powder, flour, salt, and nutmeg.
5. Into the egg mixture, stir the maple syrup and bourbon.
6. Stir in the flour mixture and nuts until you have a batter.
7. Spoon the batter into the prepared pan and even out.
8. Place into the oven and bake 50 minutes.
9. Remove from the oven and let cool in the pan 10 minutes.
10. Remove from the pan and cool on a wire rack.

Maple Walnut Pie

(Makes 1 pie)

One of the greatest American pies of all time is the seasonal pecan pie. It is simply a pie with a perfect sweetness and texture. The problem with a pecan pie, however, is the fact that, if you live outside of the South, you sometimes have to mortgage the house to buy a decent amount of pecans. Maple Walnut Pie is also delicious and will cost less than a pecan pie yet still give you that wonderful seasonal feeling.

You will notice one of the words in the title of this pie is "maple." That means you will use maple syrup. Maple syrup is the cooked sap of a tree. It is natural and quite sweet. It is not a maple-flavored corn syrup you use to ruin pancakes, waffles, or French toast. Use the real deal and enjoy the natural sweetness of Mother Nature.

The crust is a very important part of any pie. Matter of fact, a bad crust can ruin a pie. We use only one crust for most of our pies, and it is a very simple crust to make at home. It is the French pâte brisée, which is really just a fancy name for a butter crust. You can find the recipe on page 276. Maple Walnut Pie only uses a bottom crust.

Ingredients:

¾ cup maple syrup
3 eggs
6 Tbs. butter, softened
⅓ cup sugar
¼ cup brown sugar
2 cups chopped walnuts, coarse or fine
1 Tbs. vanilla
¼ tsp. ground nutmeg
1 unbaked pie crust (bottom only) (page 276)

Steps

1. Preheat your oven to 350°F.

2. In a medium saucepan over medium heat, bring the maple syrup to a boil. Reduce the heat to a simmer and cook 10 minutes. Be careful not to burn the syrup.

3. Remove the syrup from the heat and let cool.

4. In a medium bowl, whisk the eggs until thick and creamy.

5. In a mixer with the paddle attachment, beat the butter, sugar, and brown sugar for 5 minutes.

6. Add the maple syrup and eggs and beat for 5 minutes.

7. Stir in the walnuts, vanilla, and nutmeg.

8. Spoon into the pie shell.

9. Place into the oven and bake 35 minutes.

10. Remove from the oven and let cool before serving.

Mud Cake

(Makes 1 cake)

Remember venturing out into the yard as a child and making mud pies after it rained? Getting your hands all gooey and then bringing them into the house all proud and laying them before your mom? Yeah, well, Mud Cake has nothing to do with that, but I just thought I would relive a memory.

Mud Cake is a Southern cake which is still pretty popular in many areas of the South and rapidly becoming a favorite everywhere else. At one time, it was one of the most popular desserts at all roadside eateries in this area of America. The first time I ever enjoyed this dessert, I actually thought it was going to be made with . . . mud!

The dessert gets its name from its appearance. The use of cocoa powder makes it look like mud. This really is a wonderful cake—and who doesn't love a dessert topped with marshmallows? This is still a rather popular dessert at those famed Southern church dinners, and if you ever want to relive a true piece of Americana, make it for dessert for one of your Sunday family dinners.

Ingredients
½ cup butter, melted
2 cups sugar
1 cup cocoa powder, divided
½ tsp. salt
4 eggs
1 Tbs. vanilla
1½ cups flour
1½ cups chopped pecans
2 cups powdered sugar
½ cup milk
¼ cup butter, softened
1 bag miniature marshmallows

Steps
1. Preheat your oven to 350°F. Line the bottom of a 10x15-inch jellyroll pan with parchment paper.
2. In a mixer with the paddle attachment, beat the melted butter, sugar, ½ cup of cocoa, salt, eggs, and vanilla for 5 minutes.

3. Stir in the flour and pecans to form a batter.

4. Spoon the batter onto the prepared jellyroll pan and even out.

5. Place into the oven and bake 25 minutes.

6. In a mixer with the paddle attachment, beat the powdered sugar, milk, butter, and remaining cocoa until smooth and creamy. This is your frosting.

7. Remove the cake from the oven and immediately top the cake with the marshmallows.

8. Place the cake back into the oven and bake 5 minutes, allowing the marshmallows to melt.

9. Remove the cake from the oven.

10. Drizzle the cake with the frosting and let cool before slicing and serving.

Mud Pie

(Makes 1 pie)

On page 268, we played around with a delicious Mud Cake. Now, we are going to venture into the world of pies with another classic from the South: Mud Pie. Once again, this has nothing to do with the fun little splats of wet dirt you made pies with as a child. This Mud Pie does, however, indeed look like a giant mud pie!

Mud Pie is actually a peanut butter custard–like pie. Maybe the best way to describe it is to think about the inside of a Reese's® peanut butter cup yet smoother and richer. Okay, I am sure that got your attention. This is a great all-American pie and a great dish to get kids involved in the kitchen because, let's face it, what kid doesn't like to play with peanut butter?

When I make this pie, I always use my regular pie crust, and you can find that recipe on page 276. If you want a crust that is more sweet and chic, you might want to use a graham cracker crust or a crushed cookie crust (I have made it with an Oreo crust). This is fun. This is tasty. This is American!

Ingredients
¾ cup sugar
¼ cup cornstarch
¼ tsp. salt
3 cups milk
4 egg yolks
¼ cup butter, softened
¾ cup peanut butter
1 Tbs. vanilla
1 pre-baked pie crust (bottom only) (page 276)

Steps
1. In a medium saucepan over medium heat, whisk the sugar, cornstarch, salt, and milk until thickened and smooth.

2. Whisk in the egg yolks, one at a time, until well blended and smooth and bring to a simmer while whisking.

3. Reduce the heat to low, and whisk 3 minutes. You want the consistency to be that of a thick custard.

4. Remove the pan from the heat and stir in the butter, peanut butter, and vanilla.

5. Spoon the mixture into the pre-baked pie crust and bring to room temperature.
6. Chill the pie at least 1 hour before serving.

··· **Note** ···

The filling will solidify as it cools in the refrigerator.

Peach Pie

(Makes 1 pie)

It may not be the quintessential American pie, but a homemade Peach Pie certainly is the ultimate Southern pie. The first thing I always do when I hit the Georgia state line during peach season is find an orchard and make a juicy mess of myself. Yes, it is true: the best peaches come from Georgia!

I really don't know what I love best about peach pie. Is it the aroma when you slice the pie or the flavors when it enters the mouth? Peach Pie is the official pie of summer, and you will always find one in the dessert display at any diner or café during the season. The secret to the perfect Peach Pie? Fresh peaches!

If you have ever had the pleasure of eating a real peach pie at a diner or café in the South, you might have noticed it tasted a little different than what you may have been used to, and the reason is two-fold: brown sugar and buttermilk. Yes, it is Southern, so there must be buttermilk involved. The brown sugar gives the pie and the peaches a richness without taking away from their natural flavor. The buttermilk—just a touch—brings out the vibrancy in the peaches. As far as a crust for Peach Pie? In the South, it would always be a lard crust, but for me, I always use the same pie crust made with butter (and you can find that recipe on page 276).

Ingredients

5 cups peaches, peeled, pitted, and sliced
¼ cup organic peach jam
¾ cup brown sugar
¼ cup flour
¼ tsp. ground cinnamon
2-piece pie crust (top and bottom), unbaked (page 276)
2 Tbs. butter
1 Tbs. buttermilk

Steps

1. Preheat your oven to 425°F.
2. In a large bowl, toss the sliced peaches with the peach jam, brown sugar, flour, and cinnamon.
3. Let the peaches rest 15 minutes.
4. Place the peaches into the unbaked pie shell.

5. Dot the top of the peaches with the butter.
6. Place the top crust over the peaches, press the edges together, and make a few slashes in the dough to act as heat vents.
7. Brush the top crust with the buttermilk.
8. Place into the oven and bake 40 minutes.
9. Remove from the oven and let cool before serving.

Pecan Pie

(Makes 1 pie)

Among food historians, there has always been an argument about where Pecan Pie originated. There are those who say Alabama. There are those who say New Orleans. The fact of the matter is that no one knows for sure, but one thing we do know, the pecan was introduced to American cooking from the Native Americans somewhere in the South. During the holiday season (Thanksgiving through New Year's Day), most homes will, at one time or another, have a Pecan Pie sitting on the table.

There is really only one problem with real Pecan Pie, and that problem is, in order for it to be authentic, it must be made with corn syrup—and corn syrup is not one of the better things you can put into your body. However, with that noted and since Pecan Pie is usually a pie reserved for holiday occasions, eating it in moderation will not be harmful (plus it is damn delicious). There are some people who find Pecan Pie to be too sweet. Sorry, nothing can be done about that!

The best crust for a Pecan Pie is one made with either lard or butter. You can find the pie crust I use for all my pies on page 276. It is a very simple butter crust called a pâte brisée (yes, it is French).

Ingredients

1 cup corn syrup
1 cup sugar
½ cup butter
4 eggs, beaten

1 Tbs. vanilla
¼ tsp. salt
2 cups halved pecans
unbaked pie crust (bottom only)
    (page 276)

Steps

1. Preheat your oven to 350°F.

2. In a medium saucepan over medium heat, stir the corn syrup, sugar, and butter until it comes to a boil and then cook 5 minutes.

3. Remove the pan from the heat and let it cool.

4. Into the cooled syrup, whisk the eggs, vanilla, and salt.

5. Stir in the pecans.

6. Spoon the mixture into the pie shell. Place into the oven and bake 55 minutes.

7. Remove from the oven and let cool on a rack until ready to slice and serve.

Strawberries and Vanilla Kissed Cream

(Serves 4)

During the latter part of spring and all through the summer, you can't go into a decent diner, café, or roadside eatery and not see strawberries on the dessert menu. These colorful and naturally sweet, oblong, globular delights spell "summer" like no other treat from Mother Nature. Aside from the usual and delicious strawberry shortcake, you will also see the fabled Strawberries and Cream.

This particular Strawberries and Cream I had at a café in the Napa Valley of California. It is an adaptation of the usual Strawberries and Cream yet with a very definite touch of California cuisine. Instead of serving the strawberries with just sweetened cream, the chef took it one step further. The cream is a blend of cream cheese and heavy cream, kissed with a touch of vanilla. I didn't want to stop eating this dessert.

To add a touch of nouvelle cuisine, the café where I had this dish had added an interesting twist. They sprinkled the top of the dessert with black seeds (black sesame seeds), which are considered one of the most nutritious seeds you can put into your body. It adds a wonderful look to the dessert when presented and gives a nice nutty crunch. Black sesame seeds can be found in most markets and in all Asian markets.

Ingredients

8-ounce package cream cheese, softened
2 Tbs. heavy cream
2 Tbs. brown sugar

1 Tbs. vanilla
1 basket strawberries, quartered
2 tsp. black sesame seeds

Steps

1. In a mixer with the paddle attachment, beat the cream cheese and heavy cream until smooth.

2. Stir in the brown sugar and vanilla.

3. Gently fold in the strawberries.

4. Spoon the strawberries and cream into goblets or dessert dishes.

5. Sprinkle with the black sesame seeds and serve.

Pie Crust

(Makes one 9-inch pie crust)

There is a saying that goes, "Any pie is only as good as its crust." There may be more fact to this saying than fiction. Have you ever had a pie with a terrible crust? It is simply nasty. You don't want to eat the pie, no matter how good and fresh the filling may be. The crust is the home of the pie, and no one likes nor wants an ugly home.

To me, a pie crust must be so good you can eat it on its own. It should be more along the lines of a flaky pastry. It should be delicate yet have the strength to hold either a natural fruit filling or a luxurious cream filling. To make a true pie crust is a work of art, and luckily for all of us, it is an art form anyone can conquer. It may take a few times to master the pie crust, but once you do, the limits are endless.

This pie crust is commonly known in the culinary world as a pâte brisée. Yes, it is French, but don't let that scare you off. It is not only one of the most classic pie crusts in the world, it may also be one of the easiest to prepare. You probably already have all the ingredients in your kitchen, so all you'll need is a rolling pin.

Ingredients

1¼ cups flour
2 tsp. sugar
½ tsp. salt
½ cup butter, chilled and diced
4 Tbs. ice water

Steps

1. Preheat your oven to 350°F degrees.

2. In a large bowl, whisk the flour, sugar, and salt.

3. Place the butter in the bowl and, using a pastry blender, cut the butter into the flour until crumbly.

4. Gradually stir in the ice water, a half tablespoon at a time, until the dough comes together. (You might not need all of the water, depending on humidity levels in your kitchen.)

5. Place the dough on a floured surface and knead just until you can form a ball.

6. Wrap the dough in plastic and chill 15 minutes.

7. Remove the dough to a floured surface and roll out to fill your pie plate.

8. Place into the oven and bake 20 minutes.

··· **Note** ···

If your pie recipe calls for an unbaked pie shell, disregard steps 1 and 8.

··· **Note** ···

This recipe will make one pie crust (either top or bottom) for a pie 8–12 inches in diameter. To make a double crust (top and bottom), double the recipe.

Poppy Seed Bread

(Makes 1 loaf)

Poppy seeds. I know what you're thinking. You'll eat some of this then have to take a drug test for work and get fired. Well . . . not really. While eating too many poppy seeds can cause a false positive on a drug test, the actuality is that the reading will not come across as an opiate. Yes, opium does come from the same plant, but it does not come from the seeds. So, have a slice or two of Poppy Seed Bread!

When I was growing up and my family would travel, many of the diners and cafés we would visit would have this dessert bread on their menu. My mother called it "bug bread" because she thought the seeds looked like bugs. It was also for this reason that I tried Poppy Seed Bread. After all, what young boy would not want to eat something with bugs in it? Turns out, Poppy Seed Bread is a wonderful dessert bread usually served with fresh fruit. Now, when you see it in some rather chic cafés, it will be served with a dollop or two of organic yogurt. Yes, it is quite a versatile dessert bread.

Poppy seeds are not only one of the oldest food products known to man, they are also quite nutritious. Matter of fact, they are considered to be one of the more nutritious seeds you can eat and are currently being looked into for their anticancer properties. You can find poppy seeds in most markets, and they are rather inexpensive.

Ingredients

1 cup sugar
2 eggs
1 cup evaporated milk
1 cup corn oil
2 cups flour
½ tsp. baking powder
¼ tsp. salt
1 tsp. vanilla
¼ cup poppy seeds

Steps

1. Preheat your oven to 375°F. Line the bottom of a 9x5-inch loaf pan with parchment paper.
2. In a large bowl, whisk the sugar, eggs, evaporated milk, and oil.
3. In a medium bowl, whisk the flour, baking powder, and salt.

4. Stir the flour mixture into the milk mixture just until blended.
5. Stir in the vanilla and poppy seeds to make a thick batter.
6. Spoon the batter into the prepared loaf pan.
7. Place into the oven and bake 60 minutes.
8. Remove from the oven and let cool in the pan 10 minutes.
9. Remove from the pan and let cool on a wire rack.

Pumpkin Bread

(Makes 2 loaves)

There is that certain time of the year when everything under the sun has the dreaded "pumpkin spice" in it. Every food ad you read will loudly proclaim "pumpkin spice." Lies, total lies! This is really a combination of ground cinnamon, allspice, and nutmeg. There is no pumpkin to be found. Now that we've got that out of the way, let us enjoy a lovely slice of Pumpkin Bread featuring . . . pumpkin spice!

Pumpkin Bread has always been a rather popular dessert bread at many cafés. It began to gain national recognition when a rather large chain of coffee shops/stores/kiosks began to sell it with their various "pumpkin spice" liquid concoctions. Personally, I would prefer a few slices of Pumpkin Bread over pumpkin pie anytime. It is moist, it is sweet, it is spicy, and it features real pumpkin, which is a wonderful food to put into your body (we use organic canned pumpkin puree).

When making this bread (and it is very simple), you do want to stay away from the canned gunk called "pumpkin pie filling." Not good! Use an organic pumpkin puree, and then during the process of making the Pumpkin Bread, you will be adding your own spices. This recipe is for two loaves, and this is one of the few dessert breads which freezes very well.

Ingredients
3½ cups flour
1 tsp. salt
2½ cups sugar
1 tsp. baking soda
2 cups pumpkin puree
1 cup corn oil
½ cup water
4 eggs, beaten
1 tsp. ground cinnamon
½ tsp. ground nutmeg

Steps
1. Preheat your oven to 350°F. Line two 9x5-inch loaf pans with parchment paper.
2. In a large bowl, whisk the flour, salt, sugar, and baking soda.
3. In a mixer with the paddle attachment, beat the pumpkin puree, oil, water, eggs, cinnamon, and nutmeg 5 minutes on medium speed.

4. Spoon the pumpkin mixture into the flour and stir just until blended.

5. Spoon the batter into the prepared loaf pans.

6. Place into the oven and bake 90 minutes (depending on the size of your loaf pans; see note).

7. Remove from the oven and let cool in the pans 10 minutes.

8. Remove from the pans and cool on a wire rack.

··· **Note** ···

This bread does "dome" quite a bit while baking, and once it starts to cool, the dome will settle. The actual baking time does depend on the size of your bread pan and the type of metal it is constructed from. After about 65 minutes, check for doneness.

Pumpkin Spoon Bread

(Serves 6)

On page 42, I share with you a wonderful Spoon Bread which is perfect for any holiday table—or for that matter, anytime you want a wonderful soufflé-like bread. With this Pumpkin Spoon Bread, you get a wonderful dessert variation of Spoon Bread, and it is a "must" for at least one of your holiday dinner tables. Whereas Spoon Bread itself, being soufflé-like, is of French origin, this Pumpkin Spoon Bread is purely American!

Since this dish features pumpkin, you are going to have to buy some canned pumpkin (unless you want to roast and puree a whole pumpkin yourself). What you want is pure pumpkin. You do not want the gunk called "pumpkin pie filling." You want an organic pumpkin puree. You do not want any of the faux spices in the pumpkin puree. The only ingredient you want to see on the can is pumpkin (and maybe water). You will add the spices yourself as you make the Pumpkin Spoon Bread.

This dish is very reminiscent of a soufflé. This means that, in order for the full impact of the dish to be appreciated, it must be presented to the table shortly after it comes out of the oven. The heat of the oven puffs up the Pumpkin Spoon Bread. As it cools, it will deflate. This takes nothing away from the flavor.

Ingredients

1¼ cups buttermilk
1¼ cups cream
½ cup pumpkin puree
1 cup yellow cornmeal
1 tsp. ground cinnamon
½ tsp. ground nutmeg
½ tsp. salt
¼ tsp. ground white pepper
5 eggs
honey to drizzle atop (or maple syrup)

Steps

1. Preheat your oven to 400°F. Lightly oil or butter an 8x11-inch deep baking dish.

2. In a medium saucepan over medium heat, whisk the buttermilk, cream, and pumpkin puree. Cook the mixture 5 minutes while whisking (do not let it come to a boil).

3. Whisk in the cornmeal and cook 5 minutes while whisking.
4. Remove the pan from the heat and stir in the cinnamon, nutmeg, salt, and white pepper.
5. In a medium bowl, whisk the eggs until thick and frothy.
6. Stir the eggs into the pumpkin-cornmeal mixture.
7. Spoon into the prepared baking dish.
8. Place into the oven and bake 35 minutes or until it is lightly browned (the middle will be a little wobbly).
9. Serve soon after removing from the oven.

Sweet Potato Pie

(Makes 1 pie)

There has always been a burning question in my family. Is Sweet Potato Pie a dessert or a side dish? It is really an interesting question. If you go to eateries which feature Sweet Potato Pie, you will find it on either menu. If you go into Southern homes during the holiday period, you will find it served both ways. I really do not know the answer to this question, but here is how I determine how I will serve it: If I am going to top it with whipped cream, it is a dessert. If I am going to top it with marshmallows, it is a side dish.

Now for the always-asked question, "Is there a difference between a sweet potato and a yam?" The simple answer is, yes, a big difference, both botanically and nutritionally. Since this is not a science book, I won't go into the details but feel free to Google them. For Sweet Potato Pie, you want only sweet potatoes. Here is the easiest way to tell the difference in America: It is the law that they must be labeled appropriately in your local market. There, you can't mess it up!

The perfect crust for your Sweet Potato Pie is the one I always use for all my pies. It is a butter crust called a pâte brisée. Yes, it is a fancy French name, but it is also very simple to make. You can find the recipe in this section.

Ingredients

2 eggs, beaten
¾ cup sugar
5-ounce can evaporated milk
3 Tbs. butter
1 Tbs. vanilla
¼ tsp. ground cinnamon
1⅓ cups mashed sweet potatoes
1 unbaked pie crust (bottom only) (page 276)

Steps

1. Preheat your oven to 350°F.
2. In a mixer with the paddle attachment, beat the eggs, sugar, evaporated milk, butter, vanilla, and cinnamon 5 minutes.
3. Add the mashed sweet potatoes and beat an additional 5 minutes.
4. Pour the mixture into the crust.
5. Place into the oven and bake 30 minutes.

6. Line the edges of the crust with foil (to prevent burning) and bake an additional 20 minutes.

7. Remove the pie from the oven and remove the foil from the perimeter of the pie.

8. Let the pie cool before slicing and serving.

Walnut Bread

(Makes 1 loaf)

The simple fact is: dessert breads are as much a part of the American food landscape as apple pie. Okay, apple pie is not American (it's French, but you get my drift). Dessert breads were brought to America by the settlers of this great land. The chances are very strong (albeit can't be verified) that the first item out of the hearth in America was a dessert bread, and it very well may have been a simple Walnut Bread, as the settlers from England brought the famed English walnuts with them!

This dessert bread has always been a staple at cafés and coffee houses not only because it is simple and quick to make, but because it may very well be the perfect little munchie for both coffee and tea. Due to the fact that the walnuts are finely chopped, they exude more of their natural oils (flavor) into the bread while it is baking, and walnuts, for whatever reasons, just seem to marry perfectly with coffee or tea. It should also be noted that the natural oils from walnuts are also very good for your mental and physical health.

When it comes time to buy walnuts for baking and/or cooking, it is very important to remember that not all walnuts are created equal. First of all, you have various types of walnuts. The best for baking are your standard walnuts. Secondly—and I cannot stress this enough—look at the expiration date on the package. The simple fact is that very few markets check their shelves, and rancid walnuts can be fatal. Once you get your walnuts home, if you are not going to use them rather quickly, freeze them in an airtight container.

Ingredients

½ cup butter
¾ cup sugar
2 eggs, beaten
2 cups flour
2 tsp. baking powder
½ tsp. salt
1 cup milk, divided
1 cup finely chopped walnuts

Steps

1. Preheat your oven to 350°F. Line the bottom of a 9x5-inch loaf pan with parchment paper.

2. In a mixer with the paddle attachment, beat the butter, sugar, and eggs for 5 minutes.

3. In a medium bowl, whisk the flour, baking powder, and salt.

4. Beat half of the flour mixture into the butter mixture until moistened.

5. Beat in half of the milk until smooth.

6. Beat in the remaining flour mixture until moistened.

7. Beat in the remaining milk to form a batter.

8. Stir in the walnuts.

9. Spoon the batter into the prepared loaf pan.

10. Place into the oven and bake 55–60 minutes.

11. Remove from the oven and let cool in the pan 10 minutes.

12. Remove from the pan and let cool on a wire rack.

Zucchini Bread

(Makes 2 loaves)

Fact: Zucchini (a member of the squash family) is a fruit. Many fruits are made into dessert breads. Even some vegetables, such as carrots, are made into dessert breads. Dessert breads are yummy, and they are rather nutritious (as far as desserts are concerned). These are just a few of the reasons Zucchini Bread is becoming immensely popular in many of the chic cafés dotting our red-white-and-blue landscape.

There are various types of zucchini on the market today. Zucchini Bread can be made with any of them, but I find the best texture and flavor result when I use the good ol' standby zucchini we are all used to—the Italian zucchini. When it comes time to choose your zucchini, I prefer the smaller and more petite ones for this bread. I find they are less fibrous, and they tend to bake better. You can use bigger and older ones, but if you do, the baking times may be a little off. So keep an eye on them.

This recipe for Zucchini Bread will make two average-sized loaves. This is a good thing for two reasons. First, it is very hard to stop eating this (especially when slathered with some whipped cream cheese), and secondly, it freezes very well. By the way, if you don't like raisins, you can use any type of chopped dried fruit in this bread.

Ingredients

2 cups flour
1 tsp. salt
1 tsp. baking powder
1 tsp. baking soda
1 Tbs. ground cinnamon
1 tsp. ground nutmeg
3 eggs, beaten
2 cups sugar
¾ cup corn oil
2 cups grated zucchini
1½ cups finely chopped walnuts
½ cup raisins
1 Tbs. vanilla

Steps

1. Preheat your oven to 350°F. Line the bottoms of two 9x5-inch loaf pans with parchment paper.

2. In a medium bowl, whisk the flour, salt, baking powder, baking soda, cinnamon, and nutmeg.

3. In a mixer with the paddle attachment, beat the eggs, sugar, and oil for 5 minutes.

4. Stir in the zucchini, walnuts, raisins, and vanilla until combined.

5. Stir in the flour mixture just until moistened.

6. Spoon the batter into the prepared loaf pans.

7. Place into the oven and bake 50 minutes.

8. Remove from the oven and let cool in the pans 10 minutes.

9. Remove from the pans and cool on a wire rack.

Index

Conversion Charts

Metric and Imperial Conversions
(These conversions are rounded for convenience)

Ingredient	Cups/Tablespoons/ Teaspoons	Ounces	Grams/Milliliters
Butter	1 cup = 16 tablespoons = 2 sticks	8 ounces	230 grams
Cheese, shredded	1 cup	4 ounces	110 grams
Cream cheese	1 tablespoon	0.5 ounce	14.5 grams
Cornstarch	1 tablespoon	0.3 ounce	8 grams
Flour, all-purpose	1 cup/1 tablespoon	4.5 ounces/0.3 ounce	125 grams/8 grams
Flour, whole wheat	1 cup	4 ounces	120 grams
Fruit, dried	1 cup	4 ounces	120 grams
Fruits or veggies, chopped	1 cup	5 to 7 ounces	145 to 200 grams
Fruits or veggies, puréed	1 cup	8.5 ounces	245 grams
Honey, maple syrup, or corn syrup	1 tablespoon	.75 ounce	20 grams
Liquids: cream, milk, water, or juice	1 cup	8 fluid ounces	240 milliliters
Oats	1 cup	5.5 ounces	150 grams
Salt	1 teaspoon	0.2 ounce	6 grams
Spices: cinnamon, cloves, ginger, or nutmeg (ground)	1 teaspoon	0.2 ounce	5 milliliters
Sugar, brown, firmly packed	1 cup	7 ounces	200 grams
Sugar, white	1 cup/1 tablespoon	7 ounces/0.5 ounce	200 grams/12.5 grams
Vanilla extract	1 teaspoon	0.2 ounce	4 grams

Oven Temperatures

Fahrenheit	Celsius	Gas Mark
225°	110°	¼
250°	120°	½
275°	140°	1
300°	150°	2
325°	160°	3
350°	180°	4
375°	190°	5
400°	200°	6
425°	220°	7
450°	230°	8